What people are saying about …

Sweat, Blood, & Tears

"This is a good book. An honest and thoughtful book. Every young man should read this—and every man who still feels young inside should read it too."

John Eldredge, author of *Wild at Heart* and *Love & War*

"This is not only very well written, but it also engages you with its honesty and guts. Xan has found a way to speak truthfully to the longings and dilemmas of young men today. He will speak to and for many men in our world."

Richard Rohr, OFM, Men as Learners and Elders, Albuquerque, New Mexico

"After reading Xan Hood's new book, *Sweat, Blood, and Tears,* my first response came directly from my own heart as a mother: 'Xan, thank you for a book that will tell my son there is honor in being a man and there is no shame in needing help to figure out exactly what that means' … This book will be a gift that I will give to my son upon his college graduation this year—a rare gift of honor and hope! My second response to this book was as a licensed professional counselor … I see the woundedness and confusion that has come from a generation of fatherless sons. *Sweat, Blood, and Tears* fills in the gaps left by absent fathers. It honors the questions young men deserve to ask. It gives a voice to young men who have been emasculated by a culture that has encouraged girl power while offering nothing to boys ..."

Sharon A. Hersh, MA, LPC, author of
Bravehearts, The Last Addiction, and the
upcoming *Begin Again, Believe Again*

"*Sweat, Blood, and Tears* is a textured book, rich in story—a book that will call you up into the life of God. Young men do not need another book that tells them how their life should look more Christian, but a book that allows an admission of the fearfulness of entering a dangerous world with little to no instruction for their heart. Xan gives the gift of growing up before your eyes, coming to terms with his fear, desire, confusion, anger and lostness. He ... will help you not feel so alone, not so crazy for finding life so hard, not so odd for longing for so much more than the bill of goods the church has sold young men. You will feel respected by this book."

Jan Meyers Proett, counselor and author of
The Allure of Hope and *Listening to Love*

"Xan Hood has amazing capacity to open himself up to the reader. In reading *Sweat, Blood, and Tears,* I learned a lot about myself and also about life!"

Cal Turner Jr., former CEO of Dollar General

SWEAT, BLOOD, &TEARS

SWEAT, BLOOD, & TEARS

WHAT GOD USES TO MAKE A MAN

XAN HOOD

David C Cook®

transforming lives together

SWEAT, BLOOD, AND TEARS
Published by David C. Cook
4050 Lee Vance View
Colorado Springs, CO 80918 U.S.A.

David C. Cook Distribution Canada
55 Woodslee Avenue, Paris, Ontario, Canada N3L 3E5

David C. Cook U.K., Kingsway Communications
Eastbourne, East Sussex BN23 6NT, England

David C. Cook and the graphic circle C logo
are registered trademarks of Cook Communications Ministries.

The Web site addresses recommended throughout this book are offered as a
resource to you. These Web sites are not intended in any way to be or imply an
endorsement on the part of David C. Cook, nor do we vouch for their content.

All Scripture quotations, unless otherwise noted, are taken from the *Holy
Bible, New International Version*®. *NIV*®. Copyright © 1973, 1978, 1984
by International Bible Society. Used by permission of Zondervan. All
rights reserved. Scripture quotations marked MSG are taken from THE
MESSAGE. Copyright © by Eugene H. Peterson 1993, 1994, 1995, 1996,
2000, 2001, 2002. Used by permission of NavPress Publishing Group. The
author has added italics to some Scripture quotations for emphasis.

LCCN 2010925293
ISBN 978-1-4347-6681-6
eISBN 978-1-4347-0243-2

© 2010 Xan Hood
Published in association with the literary agency of Alive Communications,
Inc, 7680 Goddard St., Suite 200, Colorado Springs, CO 80920.

The Team: John Blase, Amy Kiechlin, Sarah Schultz, Erin Prater, Karen Athen
Cover Design: Juicebox Designs, Jay Smith

Printed in the United States of America
First Edition 2010

1 2 3 4 5 6 7 8 9 10

042910

Dedicated to Ron Smith

The most unlikely of ministers who in the cold stream waters
of the West has found full meaning through trout and men

Contents

While the classic European coming-of-age story generally featured a provincial boy who moved to the city and was transformed into a refined gentleman, the American tradition had evolved into the opposite. The American boy came of age by leaving civilization and striking out toward the hills. There, he shed his cosmopolitan manners and became a robust and proficient man. Not a gentleman, mind you, but a man.

Elizabeth Gilbert, *The Last American Man*

Preface

The Iliad and *The Odyssey* are coming-of-age stories. And so is *The Pilgrim's Progress*. Any time a man courageously describes the path he has walked, we are invited to join him and reckon with our journey. And our path must be appraised or it will not be lived with intentionality.

Most men seem to live lives that are lost in the daze of the day. We know, at our core, that we have not been fathered and often have failed as deeply, if not more severely, as fathers. We know the buzz of the mundane, the bombardment of the bizarre. (Seriously, I need to watch a man eat food that makes me nauseous? Or do jobs that provoke disgust? Or fish for man-eaters that remind me of bad dates?) We know the allure of the quick fix, the fast deal, and the rush of adrenaline highs. It is all so obvious and so hard to resist.

The concept of the epic journey to become a man—facing dangerous trials, suffering cowardice, rising to courage, and finding that his heart has been transformed—has been trivialized to taking a few months to roam South America with a backpack. Take the journey, learn to hop disheveled buses, drink rock-gut wine, and survive a night of food poisoning—but it is not the journey of becoming a man. After most "trips" to the wild beyond, we succumb to the predictable rhythms of the suburban-urban chic. We start a family, a career, and ease into as much comfort as we can afford.

Any other path feels too dangerous. Of course, it is even easier to pass from one task, job, or relationship to another with a wanderlust that sees rootedness as betraying the dream and succumbing to mediocrity. One path is the self-satisfied presumption and power of the older brother in Luke 15, and the other is the sensual, self-absorbed presumption of the prodigal younger brother. There is one other figure that offers an alternative way of becoming a man: the father.

I wince when I write the word *father*. I am one. It is my proudest calling. It is my deepest failure. There is no joy, no pain, no greater futility or pride, no dream, no nightmare that is deeper than my being a father. There is no forgiveness I long for more, nor accolade that will ever mean more to me than one of my children blessing me as a father. And this glorious book fathered me.

It is true of all good literature. It calls you to grieve and prize your own story. Xan allows us to watch him sweat and bleed the boisterous demands of being a gifted, entitled boy. He was sufficiently talented to simply rise in the ranks of maleness to acquire a career and a standing in his community. He could have sold out to become the "older brother." He struggles deeply with his sexuality, strutting as a poser, swift enough to drink deeply from the bog of sensual madness—he could have chosen to mirror the prodigal and still struck the pay dirt of success.

But he has chosen to become a father, a man who, in risking danger, finds in his own heart not courage, but brokenness; and in brokenness, not failure, but companionship with a God who gifts, and with other men who long to join in the seminal work of rising to be fathers. I am old enough to be Xan's father. And through his labor, I am gifted to become a man stirred by his journey to ask: "What does it mean for me to bless my father; be blessed by my children; and, most importantly, to bless my children as the man and women they are?"

I promise this book will make you laugh and weep. It will stir and trouble you. It will invite you to take your own life more seriously, but with a lightness that comes from knowing the giver of all gifts eagerly waits to show Himself in the most mundane and unexpected moments. You may walk away from reading this beautiful book with a different take. For me, I love that I have been fathered by a thirty-one-year-old man to better father my thirty-, twenty-five-, and twenty-one-year-old children.

Take up your cross, fly rod, power tools, shiny new gun, aluminum ladder, and fly vise, and follow Jesus.

Dan B. Allender, PhD,
fly fisherman, president and professor of
counseling at Mars Hill Graduate School
www.thepathlesschosen.com

Foreword

It has not always been this way. Nor does it need to always be this way. There were many great people in history, and surely some of those people had good fathers. We are in desperate need of greatness if we are to have any hope for the future, so we need to resurrect these fathers. In this lovely book, a good son offers you some very fine possibilities.

How significant that the very last words of the Hebrew Scriptures are from the prophet Malachi, who said that "a second coming" would be preceded by one who would "turn the hearts of fathers toward their children, and the hearts of children toward their fathers" (Mal. 4:26). This could be considered a brilliant segue passage between the Old and New Testaments that is still, centuries later, awaiting fulfillment. Today we need a second coming of fathers and sons.

Xan Hood offers you a very personal, well written, and compelling entranceway into the conversation between fathers and sons, and men in general. He knows the terrain, even as a young man, by reason of his own experience, passion for the cause, and years of active involvement in helping young men find their manhood, their power, and their father energy—because often they did not get it from their own fathers, who did not get it from their fathers, who did not get it from their fathers …

You can only hand on *what* has been given to you and *how* it was given to you. But there is a space for wonderful exception and possibility! Some would call it the "space for grace," or liminal space, and there are many sons who seek such grace, such healing, and such wisdom. Xan Hood is one of these men, and just like Malachi promised, he is turning the hearts and minds of the men who will listen and turn toward one another. Get ready to be turned!

Richard Rohr,
author of *Adam's Return* and *From Wild Man to Wise Man*
Albuquerque, New Mexico

ENTRANCE

WEST

The mountains are calling, and I must go.

John Muir

I never attended my college graduation.

I told my parents not to make the three-hour drive to Knoxville for the ceremony at The University of Tennessee. They were justifiably offended and disappointed. It was my college graduation, a time for great celebration. But I refused their pleading by explaining that I forgot to order the black gown.

It worked. The massive ceremony, held in a coliseum packed with 10,000 ecstatic parents and students, went on without me. I didn't want to sit through a commencement address or attend my friends' parties. All I wanted to do was sleep.

I was supposed to have been intellectually, spiritually, and academically prepared for this occasion by many professors, teachers, and ministry leaders over the past few years of my life. But I didn't feel ready. In fact I was terrified. Graduation was supposed to be some grand announcement to the world and my family that my schooling was finally complete, but I was far from being an independent man. I could not celebrate what did not ring true.

I don't even really remember choosing to go to college or why I decided on The University of Tennessee. I think I did it because it was what you did; it was a four-year stop on my way through "the system." College was as inevitable as being born, getting a driver's license, and dying. I just wasn't ready for the inevitability of it coming to an end. I just wanted to hibernate, maybe wake in a few weeks—or months.

Without understanding all the implications of growing up privileged, I was raised in an upper-class family in Brentwood, a booming suburb right outside of Nashville, Tennessee. In Brentwood the median income of families was well into the six figures and the average home price was over half a million dollars. Urban sprawl ran rampant: New strip malls were erected, neighborhoods swallowed up centuries-old farmlands, churches frequently expanded their sanctuaries, and commercial developments were as common a sight as gas-guzzling SUVs.

The accents were perfect—a little Southern drawl but not too redneck. The tea was sweet and the charm was sweeter. The soft rolling hills were delicately packed with privately owned, perfectly manicured one-acre custom homes in which one could safely raise a family. Brentwood had become home to country music stars like Kenny Chesney, Dolly Parton, and Alan Jackson. It was here they wrote their songs about family and the good life. I don't know how, but in Brentwood the concrete never cracked, weeds never grew, and dirt never collected. Litter was unheard of, trailer homes and parks nonexistent. Open spaces were reserved for country clubs and golf courses, many of which I played.

Church, work, school, and play interlaced sweetly and subtly like the crust of an apple pie—so seamlessly, in fact, that I thought God had His hands in just about everything in Brentwood. I was sure this was the life all Americans dreamed of giving their families.

Brentwood's money and success bred a host of expectations, spoken and unspoken, in the children who played in the culs-de-sac. Status, income, and education were of upmost importance. The way of Brentwood was "work smarter, not harder." Getting a top-notch education and using it were the keys to becoming a man. Private prep schools were as common as grocery stores. My parents and many others felt strongly that they were to do all they could to give their kids a better life than they had; that included providing their kids with unique opportunities for them to get ahead. My parents did their jobs and I did mine: concentrating in school so one day I could find a good job and do the same for my kids.

One bright and beautiful day in Brentwood, my dad had a professional photographer capture us standing in the backyard of our suburban house, near the newly completed pool-house addition with pink flowers in full bloom. Our family dog obediently sat by our side. My Ralph Lauren Polo shirt was white, my face and arms were tan, and my hair was gelled with an attitude of pride.

Like many other Brentwood family portraits, it was placed in a gold frame and hung in our living room, a living testimony to our family's hard-earned success. The photographer liked our image so well he hung it in the large picture window of his studio: a portrait of the good life in Brentwood. We were the all-American family, and I thought I was well on my way to becoming the all-American male.

Then came graduation.

While my parents had hopes of launching me into responsible adulthood, I was struggling. I had lived securely under the family plans: phone, car insurance, health insurance, Internet, and the college degree. All of a sudden I was being asked to make my own way, find my own plan. I think it might have been the first moment in my twenty-two years in which something was about to be required and expected of me.

In the midst of all this, I had been reading a book by John Eldredge, *Wild at Heart.* Chapter after chapter discussed masculinity, the need to rethink our experiences as men, and God's intent for manhood. The backdrop for the book was Eldredge's journey out West, one full of adventure, elk hunting, and most of all, God. It was a far cry from my Southern-gentleman, nice-guy persona and pink Polo shirts. The book struck a chord in me. It spoke about what society had lost and what I had not experienced and received as a boy in Brentwood. Welling up within me was a desire for something deeper than that gold-framed, manufactured image of life in the suburbs.

Within months of reading the book, I flew to Colorado to attend one of Eldredge's mountain retreats for men. Speakers shared their stories about God's fathering and initiating them, much of which had taken place in the context of mountains and streams and hunting and fishing. The weekend sessions explored a man's wounds, his need for healing, and finding his place in creation. I heard nothing about hair gel or brunch. It became clear that I had not matured and developed the way these men had. I had not been tested physically or emotionally, not in the ways a man needed to be. I could relate to the words Henry David Thoreau had penned in his journal: "I cannot but feel as if I lived in a tamed and, as it were, emasculated country … a tribe of Indians that had lost all its warriors."[1]

I had never been around men so open and vulnerable, a room of 400 sharing their hearts—with tears. Men broken over their life stories and wanting God to speak to their masculinity. They looked at me with desperate eyes, as if to say, "If only I knew all of this at your age." I felt like I had discovered real men—real warriors.

While in Colorado Springs I also met a girl: Jayne. She was standing behind the pastry display at Starbucks. I approached her and we quickly connected. She was winsome, bright-eyed, and glimmering. She was also new to the area, having just moved to Colorado from Pennsylvania a few weeks before.

I flew back to Knoxville feeling like a new man. Struggling to find my way, I worked a few part-time jobs that summer, all the while dreaming of places beyond Brentwood—places far out West, past Kansas and her cornfields to the edge of God's country, where mountains suddenly rose and rivers ran through them.

Before long, Jayne decided to move to Knoxville so we could date, and soon after, I had the sense that God was leading us to marriage. Within a year we'd made it official. And so the fortunate son and his new bride went west to Colorado, toward God's rugged mountain terrain and teary-eyed warriors who might be willing to help a boy become a man.

1

GEAR

You would be amused to see me, broad sombrero hat, fringe and
beaded buckskin shirt, horse hide *chaparajos* or riding trousers,
and cowhide boots, with braided bridle and silver spurs.

Theodore Roosevelt

I had always heard that Theodore Roosevelt was a tough, hardy
"man's man" sort of guy: a hunter, outdoorsman, activist, soldier,
explorer, naturalist, and "rough rider." But it wasn't always so. Much
like me, he was raised a refined, tame city boy, a member of a wealthy,
powerful family with political influence. He was a sickly, asthmatic
youngster who at the age of twenty-three still appeared boyish and
underdeveloped. Both the press and his fellow New York state
assemblymen made light of his high-pitched voice and "dandified"
clothing, calling him names like "Jane-Dandy" and "Punkin-Lily."[2]
He was what we now refer to as a "pretty boy."

Photos Courtesy of Theodore Roosevelt Collection, Harvard College Library[3]

It seems Theodore knew he needed to escape the confines of the city, to be tested and initiated beyond his Jane-Dandy world. There was only one direction to go: west.

"At age twenty-five, on his first trip to the Dakota badlands in 1883, Roosevelt purchased a ranch, bought a herd of cattle, hired ranch hands, and, spending considerable time there, began to develop his Western image."[4] It is said he took rides "of seventy miles or more in a day, hunting hikes of fourteen to sixteen hours, stretches in the saddle in roundups of as long as forty hours," pushing himself physically and mentally.[5]

Within two weeks of moving to Colorado, I drove up alone to the Orvis store in Denver to purchase a complete set of official Orvis gear: waders, boots, vest, and a fly rod. I had come to the West to bond with earth, wind, and rivers that I could fly-fish—and to find God. The fishing needed to be done in official Orvis gear—only the best.

You see, coming from a town of status and wealth, the type of gear you chose was very important. It needed to function, but it also needed to make you look good so you could feel good while looking good.

In my eyes Orvis was the status symbol of real and serious fly fishermen, the hallmark of class. I stocked up on floatant, little boxes, nippers, and line—all Orvis products and logos, of course. I paid with a new credit card and walked out.

While Theodore would become a great, brave man, his first attempts out West were about as comical as my own. It is written that he "began to construct a new physical image around appropriately virile Western decorations and settings." These photographs show him posing "in a fringed buckskin outfit, complete with hunting cap, moccasins, cartridge belt, silver dagger, and rifle."[6] In a letter to his sister back East, he bragged, "I now look like a regular cowboy dandy, with all my equipments finished in the most expensive style."

Photos Courtesy of Theodore Roosevelt Collection, Harvard College Library[7]

Though he looks like a young man in a Halloween costume, something much deeper than child's play was occurring. A rich city boy was exploring another side of himself. The costumes, however foolish they appeared at the time, were a part of this becoming and would, in time, become him.

I was also searching for a new image, one more closely connected with nature. In his book *Iron John*, Robert Bly writes, "Some say that the man's task in the first half of his life is to become bonded to matter: to learn a craft, become friends with wood, earth, wind, or fire."[8] I had yet to experience that. Ralph Lauren Polo shirts and a posh lifestyle were simply not enough. And while it's likely that neither of us could have verbalized it at the time, Theodore and I were learning that a man had to find something away from all of it. I think his fringed buckskin and my Orvis gear were safe compromises between the worlds we were straddling.

A week after I bought my Orvis gear, I drove about an hour away to the South Platte River. An Internet search revealed that I could quickly access it from the road. On my way I stopped at a little fly shop in Woodland Park, Colorado. A retired-looking man had blessed my obvious naïveté but left the teaching to a sheet of paper, diagrammed for a nymph-dropper rig. He made a few fly suggestions and sent me on my way with the paper and a pat on the back. It was time to become Brad Pitt: Orvis-endorsed, perched on a rock, waiting for a fish.

I arrived on the water's edge at about 2 p.m. Like a warrior dressing for battle, I donned my Orvis gear and set to work on the nymph-dropper rig. About an hour later, after clamping on weights, indicator, and tying two flies onto the razor-thin line, it looked like I'd tied my grandmother's collection of jewelry to a string. I stood in the middle of the river, flung the line out, and whipped it back and forth, feeling good and enjoying the four-count rhythm.

Though I filled the hours with flipping and whipping, I could not seem to hook a fish. *Were they in the rapids? The calm water? Should I cast upstream or downstream?* The paper didn't say. It didn't help that every few minutes I would get caught on a branch, or grass or algae would get on the flies, tangling them with knots. It was getting dark, and I was getting lonely and frustrated at Orvis, God, and myself.

But there came a last minute hope: I remembered Dan Allender telling a story at a leadership conference about going fly-fishing with his son. As an unsuccessful day of fishing came to a close, he told his son they needed to call it a day. But his son kept fishing, and then, on the fifth and final cast, as all hope was fading like the sun—BAM!—a massive trout on his fly rod. It was a miracle. Dan concluded his speech with this lesson: "God is the God of the fifth cast … He comes through in the end."

And so I began my count. *Okay, Lord,* I prayed. *This is for You. Help me fish. Catch me a trout.* One cast … nothing. Second cast … nothing. Third cast … nothing. Cast again … nothing. God of the fifth cast … not for me. Eleventh? Nope. I kept going. God of the seventeenth cast … God of the twenty-second cast …

Before long, darkness covered me, and I could no longer see my orange indicator. It was over. There would be no fish that day.

I stood all alone in the middle of the river, holding my empty net. There wasn't a soul in sight—not a fish, not even God. It was haunting. I demanded an explanation. *Where are the fish? Where are You? Just one, God. All I wanted was one. One simple fish would have made this day worth it.*

Would God not give a man dressed in Orvis a fish if he asked?

2

MORE

I wandered the long narrow aisles stocked with canned foods
and cloth, dry goods and work boots, tools and shotguns,
colognes and wallpaper. Unable to decide, I walked and walked,
touching everything as if it held some wonderful mystery.

Harry Middleton, *The Earth Is Enough*

I wish I had nothing else to say about my equipment obsession, that
my affair with Orvis gear was the extent of it. But it's simply not true,
nor was I content to just fly-fish. Mountains, hills, trails, and wide-
open spaces surrounded me. And in order to truly enjoy them, you
need a lot of gear. Stuff I never needed before became as necessary as
food, water, and oxygen.

I began to acquire gear like a developer acquires property: a
mountain bike, then a road bike (one for my wife too), tents, back-
packs, stoves, sleeping bags, snowshoes, North Face jackets, and

Mountain Hardware rain pants. I would walk the aisles of REI and just grab stuff. Or go to the store's Saturday "garage sales" of half-off used gear and buy a third backpack—just in case.

I had the same problem with tools. I had started my own painting company in Colorado—really a pathetic attempt at a business, an easy way to make fast cash. I often found myself wandering into places like Home Depot, drooling over the selection of Ridgid, Ryobi, Milwaukee, and DeWalt tools that promised to transform me into the man I was trying to unearth. There were sanders. Lathes. Routers. High-impact drills. Reciprocating saws. Circular saws. Chop saws. Mitre saws. Accessories, too, like the twenty-nine-piece DeWalt drill set that complemented my DeWalt 14.4-volt cordless power drill. I just had to have it.

No reason to buy a tool was too shallow. I remember one painting job that entailed installing a chair rail: basically a few feet of trim on a wall. My hammer, a box of a finish nails, and a cheap plastic mitre box would have done the trick. But it seemed a great excuse to finally get the DeWalt heavy-duty twelve-inch compound mitre saw along with the Porter-Cable three-nailer and compressor combo kit. (It came with staple gun, too.) The purchase cost as much as what I made in painting a few rooms in the house. And I easily justified it.

I felt a great wonder while buying these gadgets, from tearing through the box to wielding them in my hands. They represented power, mastery, ownership, masculinity—symbols of what I wanted inside me. It was as if buying a new tool or piece of gear brought me closer to who I hoped to become—and further from the man I was out East.

Let me say that I never felt good buying the stuff. I knew I was an impressionable consumer susceptible to impulse buying. But that realization didn't stop me as our bank account dwindled and the credit card bills piled up. I kept my wife in the dark about most of it. I would always leave the store feeling like crap, carrying the shame and thinking, *I did it again.* There was this sense of foolishness about what I was doing, but it almost felt like I couldn't help it. I had collected a garage full of tools and gear. And I had yet to start a real job—or even catch a fish.

3

TEARS

With initiators gone from our culture, we do not
receive instruction on … going into grief … but one
sometimes feels that in the United States a man
is supposed to feel grief only at a funeral.

Robert Bly, *Iron John*

I was sitting with my wife, Jayne, on the couch one night when she
looked at me and said, "I've never seen your tears."

Hmm … tears. Well, let's see. I flipped through my memory while
she stared at me. *Tears? Crying?* I was trying to think back, but nothing was coming. I was digging deep, hoping to give some reason for
her to take me off the hook. We looked at each other, and I really
didn't know what to say.

"Really, honey?" I asked. "Are you sure?"

"Oh, I am sure."

It felt weird to admit, but she was right. I had never cried in front of her. To be honest, I had not cried much at all over the past few years. Not around my friends. Or my parents. Or anyone, really.

It was weird to think that way because I wasn't a hard or violent man, not the leathery, thick–skinned, violent, emotionless type of *Dirty Harry* personality. In fact some people had labeled me as more of a sensitive type, a nice guy. So something in me had assumed I was pretty good at expressing emotions. But maybe not. She was right. I hadn't shed a lot of tears, even on my own.

I sat there, unsure of what to say and feeling awkward. Of course I didn't want to cry, not that I could anyway. I don't know exactly where it came from, but I'd always believed men don't cry much. I mean, how many times have you seen men cry? Maybe men going through times of pain and brokenness—maybe. While a part of me knew it was probably a good thing to do, the other parts of me saw it more as weakness.

I found this was true of other guys. They, too, found it difficult to get to that place of grief and tears. My friend Ryan had confessed he had never been able to cry. He always thought men weren't supposed to cry. He remembered being at a friend's funeral surrounded by crying people, men included. While everyone around him was crying, he recalls thinking, *I should be crying right now. I am at a funeral. Why can't I cry? I'm supposed to be crying!* "So I tried to squeeze them out," he told me. "I mostly tried to talk myself into crying by reminding myself that I was at a funeral, that someone close to me had died. But it didn't work."

I had always associated tears with femininity. The thought of tears took me to tenderness, love, nurturing, and care. As a boy and

young man, I had rarely, if ever, seen men cry. And when you are a
kid trying to make it in a world of men, crying almost seems like letting down your guard, being exposed to something weak that other
men don't do.

Without a whole lot of masculine things to cling to, crying felt
like it might forever banish me from masculinity. As Mary Sykes
Wylie writes in *Panning for Gold*, "Any show of gentleness or 'soft-
ness' was unmanly and would be met with harsh punishment and
brutal public humiliation."[9] Many of our fathers never showed us
their tears. One friend shared that after a fight with his brother or
a rough day at school, he would cry in his room. His father would
come home, enter his room, and say, "Real cowboys don't cry, son."
Then he would walk out.

Ryan, the young man who could not cry at the funeral, had a
similar experience with his father. As a young boy he was crying on
his bed after he witnessed his parents fighting. His father tried to get
him to quit but only frightened him more. Frustrated, his father said,
"I'll give you something to cry about," and gave his nine-year-old
son a punch in the gut. It was the last time Ryan ever remembered
crying. He confessed to me, "I feel emotionless."

While my wife had never seen my tears, she had seen my anger. In
fact I had karate chopped a few items from our home, taken out a
wooden laundry rack, flipped over a coffee table twice, kicked a hole
in our laundry room door, threw a glass candleholder through the
wall, and broke a lamp when we were fighting. It was weird to experience so much anger after getting married. While I could not cry, I

seemed to be enraged, and I wasn't sure over what. Little things, like driving in the car or a conversation with my wife, would set me off. I was feeling alone out in Colorado and trying to make sense of it all.

If I was honest, I was angry with a lot of things. My past had left me short of what I needed to mature. I was angry with people in general—and at God more often than I wanted to admit. I was angry with my mom. My dad. The church. My wife. A few people in Knoxville. An old mentor. Gosh, often my life in general. And while sometimes that anger was directed outward, I internalized most of it. I didn't scream in public, give people dirty looks, or throw fits. I was more discreet. I let it out in ways that allowed me to feign cool and keep others out of it. I could seethe for hours, obsessively thinking about a situation, something, or someone. And while I don't know how, the anger often settled, lost its steam, and leveled off. I would go about my day until it again reared its ugly head.

While I wasn't aware of it at the time, even the music I listened to had a bit of a rebel yell in it. I didn't need dark goth stuff, but I did appreciate the gruff, masculine voices of Bono and Eddie Vedder. Their voices had this frustration and angst that gave voice to the emotions I could not feel. It explained my struggle with so much of the popular soft worship music. It was too smooth, too sweet. Too meek and mild—too happy. God was always good, and we were always supposed to be smiling with a sweet-sounding voice. But sometimes I just wanted to throw my Bible at the stage and say, "I don't feel like that! I want to put on boxing gloves and fight God right now, not cuddle up with a pillow and blanky." But I never did that; I was too nice.

A nice guy who was steaming inside.

My friend Matthew, probably the nicest guy you could ever meet, once shared that during the workweek, there are times he wants to flip out at his desk—pound his computer screen into pieces, fling his keyboard across the room, topple tables. Though he often bottles it up and flashes a friendly smile, the anger is there, threatening to erupt.

Another friend, Ben, for years went by the nickname "Gentle Ben" because of his calm and tender personality. But he admits that since being married, he feels more anger than gentleness. Thinking about it, he said, "How can Gentle Ben coexist with all this anger?" Another friend, Forrest, took his anger out in the boxing ring during college. He was a charming and likeable Christian role model. But when he fought in the fraternity boxing tournament, he would flip this switch and let his rage explode, crushing people with his inner pain. He could switch it on and off. Those who knew him outside of the ring would have never known; he was such a good guy.

Dan Allender, the fifth-cast guy, says if you have met a man, you have met an angry man; that because of sin and the fallen world and the curse, man is a raging machine ready to destroy. Dan says just to say the word *man* really means "angry." It made sense that there were all these nice-guy Christian personalities who were angry, most of whom, like me, had no idea.

I was an angry dude who had no idea how to cry, catch a trout, or take a job: all reasons to be even angrier.

4

RITUAL

Every year, 15 million licensed hunters head into America's forest
and fields in search of wild game. In New York State alone, roughly
half a million hunters harvest around 190,000 deer in the fall deer
hunting season—that's close to eight million pounds of venison.

Steven Rinella, *New York Times* columnist

During the nineteenth century, grandfathers and uncles lived in
the house, and older men mingled a great deal. Through hunting
parties, in work that men did together in farms and cottages, and
through local sports, older men spent much time with young men
and brought knowledge of male spirit and soul to them.

Robert Bly, *Iron John*

Within a few weeks of moving to Colorado Springs, Jayne and I
began attending an Anglican church at the suggestion of a friend. It

seemed a great fit. As the months rolled by, it was a place we were starting to call home.

A couple from the church, Steve and Lisa, invited us over for dinner one evening. But this wasn't any old meal—Steve called it "wild game night." It was a sort of ritual he had been practicing with his hunting buddies for years. They would get together and grill their meat from the previous year's hunts. This year Steve wanted us to join them. I was pretty excited and surprised I was invited, since I'd never killed anything with a gun or hunted.

We showed up with our offering: a fruit salad. I noticed all the women gathered in the kitchen; it was apparent I was to join the men in the backyard around the grill.

I walked to the back patio and was welcomed into the gathering of men. There was the grill master, Mark—the point man with the tongs. Charles stood next to him, then a park ranger named Paul. They seemed eager to tell me their stories, explain why they wrapped bacon around the quail, and hint at something called a "chucker." I felt like a welcomed guest. Maybe my fruit offering *was* enough.

The word *camaraderie* describes what I saw. These men were comrades, bound by a rare commodity: male friendship. As I pointed to each type of meat, I was given a hunt briefing laced with memories and laughs.

We joined the ladies and sat down to eat. When the men prayed and thanked God for the food He provided, it sounded like a real prayer—or at least what one should sound like from men who had actually seen God and their aim bring it down. As we stuffed our faces, I realized my distance. These men had a direct gratitude for the meat they killed and the experiences that strengthened their friendship.

I think I was about twelve years old when I finally realized that meat did not just show up in squares and circles, tubes, and moldable chunks. It was a shocker to learn that steak had to be cut from the body of the cow and bacon stripped from the fat of a pig. I never knew because all I ever saw were *pieces* of meat, cooked or microwaved and served on my plate. They never mooed, swam, or cackled. It never even hit me that the red color showing through the clear cellophane was actually blood. Gross.

The truth is I had been killing animals for awhile. (Or at least eating them.) They never looked like dead animals. Ever since I was two, I had been munching on McDonald's golden-brown chicken nuggets, chicken meat that had been injected into such a beautiful, round shape. Hot dogs from Oscar Mayer were so nicely rounded. And hamburgers, too. So I performed some calculations based on data I found on the People for Ethical Treatment of Animals' Web site. I wondered how many animals I had killed by age twenty-seven, assuming I was an average food eater.

I had eaten:

> *4 full cows*
> *905 chickens*
> *10 pigs*
> *30 turkeys*
> *2 ducks*
> *1,710 fish*

I didn't count those beach vacations during which I stuffed my face with shrimp. I probably ate twenty-five in one sitting, bumping the total up another hundred or so a year by my own accounting.

My math added up to around 5,200 lives that were sacrificed for me to live and eat. I had killed more animals than some wars had casualties. The tragedy is that I killed them without even knowing it. Behind my meals was a holocaust of death—one I had participated in without realizing it. As a sign of my supposed gratefulness, I would routinely offer some trite little prayer—something like "bless this food"—before I consumed my molded patties of beef. I had never offered thanks for the life that was taken or felt grateful that an animal gave up its life so I could eat. Not to mention that I had never seen one of those 5,200 animals die. All those years someone else on some farm far away had raised, fed, cleaned up after, caught, decapitated, butchered, gutted, and ground those animals, putting the meat in a hot dog tube or slicing it to fit my dinner plate.

As I looked at these men and their friendship, their smiles and full bellies, I realized I needed to participate in the cycle of life and death. I had bought into the American notion that to be given a warm bag of prepared food in exchange for the swipe of a plastic card is the most efficient transaction and a freeing one—one that allows us to go about our lives and do something more productive.

Yes, there are some pros. Efficiency and productivity allow us to focus on other forms of work. But the cons are worse. We have removed ourselves from a cycle that has been a part of this planet since the dawn of man. We have left food gathering and preparation to others. It wasn't until seeing these men, hearing their laughter, and tasting their kills that I missed something I had never known—the experience and the mystery of what it might teach me.

Maybe I was regressing, turning into a caveman or something worse. But there seemed something deeply spiritual around that dinner table. And while I did not know how, or with who, or what animal, or with what weapon, I knew I wanted to hunt. I wanted to be around men and kill an animal, to clip off its wings, maybe cut off its head, slice the fur of its body, pull out the guts, butcher the thing, and turn it into a piece of meat. Cook it on the grill. Put it on a bun with some ketchup. And sit down with Jayne and eat it.

5

ROOTS

He will be like a tree planted by the water that sends
out its roots by the stream. It does not fear when heat
comes; its leaves are always green. It has no worries
in a year of drought and never fails to bear fruit.

Jeremiah 17:8

After moving to Colorado I began painting houses part-time. (I'd picked up painting after graduating in Knoxville.) I found I could make large chunks of money in a short amount of time. We were also living off some money from the sale of my college house in Knoxville, Jayne's work at Starbucks, and a few credit cards. I figured it was a matter of time before my perfect job would find me, though I had no idea what it might be.

I had also been meeting with a mentor named John. His mentorship had consisted of counseling in his office and advice over meals.

I was sitting with him one morning when he was asked me, "Xan, what are you doing during the day? How are you supporting Jayne?" I was really unsure of what to say. I felt foolish. I mumbled a few things under my breath.

"So your wife is working and you are not?" he asked.

It embarrassed me to even think of it that way, but it was true. He paused a little as I sat in the silence of my own shame. I kind of knew what was about to come. The truth was I had heard it a lot from folks, about how I wasn't really working. I could feel their sense of, "Go get a job. Go to work. Just work somewhere, you pathetic, spoiled kid. Who cares if it's not your dream for this season?" But he spoke it more kindly.

"Xan, I feel like you are this blossoming tree with beautiful flowers," he said. "But the problem is you don't have any deep and thick roots for it to stand up. You need to go find your roots."

"Roots?"

"Yeah, roots."

While I was disappointed, there was a dignity he gave me—and an appeal to do something about it. I had never heard someone talk so kindly, acknowledge that there was something good hiding inside of me that needed development. I wanted roots and real respect—and I didn't want them just handed to me. But I was scared to settle into a mundane job "below my talents."

I sunk down in the couch, as if an epic struggle had culminated in that moment of honesty. I had spent a lot of time avoiding and running from responsibility, but I knew he was right; there was nowhere else to run.

I looked at him and agreed. "Yes, I need a job—a full-time job," I said. "Yes, probably forty hours a week. And doing something I could not try to run or manage. A regular eight-to-five job as a worker."

You have to understand that I had started a lucrative lawn-mowing business at age thirteen. I rode around on my bike, attaching flyers on mailboxes in my ritzy neighborhood. By sixteen I was making forty-five dollars for one lawn, about an hour's worth of labor: forty-five dollars an hour.

I knew how to work the system, appealing to parents by putting flyers on the mailboxes with quotes like, "Help me pay for college." It was as big a line as any; I knew very well I was never going to have to pay a dime for higher education. The money was for my own pleasure. I wasn't looking to expand the business to twenty yards a week or anything; I wasn't paying bills. I needed enough to keep some cash in my pocket and free time on my hands to do what I wanted to do.

While my friends worked summer construction jobs at four dollars and twenty-five cents an hour, slaving away with working class men, I was cutting my four or five lawns, working four or five hours, and making much more than them. I figured I had outsmarted the system. I worked at my pace, when I wanted to, and for big cash. And while it may have looked like I was a model worker, the truth was I hated work. Mowing was my way of getting out of it. My dad saw this and tried as best he could to make me work a full-time job in the summers, especially during college, but the question I always had was, "Why?" He willingly pushed himself in high school and college, working in the steel mills and lumberyards of Ohio. But as to my question, my dad didn't have an answer. It was a question his generation never asked. They just worked hard.

I shared my work scenario with my buddy Cory. I was stressed, confused about where to go and what to do for work. He had been working as an estimator with a commercial painting contractor and thought I might be able to get a job with his company. Since I had already been painting for myself and knew a thing or two, it seemed a perfect fit. I called the owner, Mike, and asked if we could meet.

I had met Mike a few times. He was a no-nonsense, highly driven man with a soft heart, but you did not want to cross him. He worked hard and played hard, and expected the same from Cory and his crew.

We chatted over burritos. Like a Catholic might confess to a priest, I reviewed my past history with work, how I had avoided it for so long, and how I would appreciate a job painting homes for him. I was not that interested in making a whole lot of money, I said, but I did need to put in forty hours a week.

He seemed amused at my requests. He let me know that forty hours a week would be the least I would be working. And I was not to start as a painter, but as a laborer. If I was to learn, I would have to start from the bottom like all of the rest. His offer was eight dollars an hour.

I shook his hand. We had a deal. And for the first time in my twenty-seven years, I had a real, full-time job.

6

WORK

God is presented to us in our Scriptures as a worker, a maker.
In the beginning, God went to work ... The spiritual life begins,
seriously begins, when we get a job and go to work.

Eugene Peterson, *Leap Over a Wall*

I pulled up to the job site like a kid on his first day of school. Instead of new tennis shoes and a shiny lunch box, I wore new, stark-white Dickies painter pants and carried my plastic blue bin of tools, rollers, and brushes. I left my car eager to earn the approval of this new breed of men. I imagined running down a long tunnel to a football field—or, umm, the job site—surrounded by scores of cheering fans. I envisioned firm handshakes and hollers from guys named Frank, Bob, and Jim, who were wearing hard hats and flannel shirts, slapping me "atta boys."

To be tested and tried among hard-laboring men was an experience I had not yet had. But I was hopeful I'd get something more than just eight bucks an hour out of this job, maybe even some form of initiation into the world of real men. And those roots I needed.

I opened my car door to find a man named John staring at me. He was near the painting van pulling out canvas drop cloths. His expression was blank. Standing near him was his son, Jack, a seventeen-year-old who had left his formal education for real-world work. John waded into the awkwardness with a stern question: "You ever painted before?"

"Oh yes, I have been painting on my own for the past few years, mostly interior jobs," I said, speaking with poise and confidence. I wanted them to know what kind of guy they were dealing with, as in, "No rookie here, fellas … You've got a gen-u-wine painter in your midst." I heard some laughter and a snicker.

And so my day began.

When I worked at a clothing store in Knoxville's upscale mall, the first days were filled with extensive training: videos about clothing items, corporate rules, expectations, and an entire safety presentation on how to use a twelve-foot ladder. I spent half an hour filling out paper forms. When the manager introduced me to the box cutter with a razor blade on the end of it, she acted as if the thing was a loaded weapon of danger. Then I shadowed an employee for a day.

But this wasn't the mall. The boss, Mike, wasn't even there yet. No friendly introductions. No paperwork to sign. A short, stocky Latino named Carlos asked if I had tools. I was instructed to grab the masking tape and start taping trim in the basement. In less than sixty seconds I was on my hands and knees prepping a room to paint by myself. It would have been nice to shadow someone. Then again, I had told them I was a veteran painter.

When I finished taping, the guys gave me a five-gallon bucket of something yellow and an armful of canvas drop cloths. Within an hour I was painting and rolling the downstairs room. I had rolled many walls; I didn't need help from them. It's paint. A roller. Moving it back and forth. A caveman could do it.

But whatever glorious dream I had of hearing "atta boy" was quickly jarred by John's voice from across the room.

"Dry!"

I could barely understand him; it sounded more like he was commanding a dog. I remained quiet and kept rolling. Then I heard it again.

"Dry!"

"Are you talking to me?" I finally asked.

He spoke like I was stupid: "Yoooouuuuurrr rrrroooollllllllll-eeeeerrrrr iiiiiiiiiisssssssss drrrryyyy."

Carlos graciously took my roller and explained that I wasn't putting enough paint on my roller when I dipped it in the bucket. It was making a sticky sound on the wall, a sign I wasn't painting properly.

The whole crew stopped what they were doing and inspected my work. It was decided the entire basement had been incorrectly painted—the old paint was bleeding through. I screwed up things that entire week, and John let me know it. Carlos was continually stopping what he was doing to explain the fundamentals of painting. Friday came and Mike arrived for a final inspection. He walked around the house like a raging bull, completely embarrassed of our work. I had forgotten to dust under the tape I laid on the baseboard;

when it pulled up, I saw the paint had bled through. He was yelling at everyone. I raised my hand and apologized to the whole crew, confessing it was probably me.

I was coming to the reality that I had no idea how to paint. In fact, as my boss reminded me, he did not hire me as a painter, but a laborer. I think everyone got a kick out of seeing the "experienced painter" taken down a couple of notches.

Everyone, that is, but me.

7

ART

My father was very sure about certain matters
pertaining to the universe. To him, all good things—
trout as well as eternal salvation—come by grace and
grace comes by art and art does not come easy.

Norman Maclean, *A River Runs Through It*

Our church had announced a fly-fishing weekend retreat in Estes
Park, Colorado: Men at the River. The organizer, Corb, had a neigh-
bor with a family cabin there and had convinced him to host a bunch
of rookie church fishermen over the weekend. It sounded like a great
experience. And I needed the help.

Any visions of a grand lodge tucked into a deep forest of pines
evaporated when I saw the radiating lime green cabin in front of us.
The place was old—really old. But it was quaint, with glass picture
windows that revealed a yellowish light coming from the kitchen. A

group of men had already arrived and were packed together, hovering over someone seated at the table. I soon saw it was an older man, beads and feathers scattered around him, tying a fly with a small metal vice.

Ron looked to be in his late fifties. He resembled an old NASCAR legend, with his bushy mustache and deep voice. His spirit was charming; a warm glow radiated from his eyes. He seemed genuinely pleased we were there and introduced us to his other fishing buddies, Gary and Vern. Each man, including Ron, had fifty years of fly-fishing experience on these waters in Rocky Mountain National Park.

Midway through tying a black jujube, he pointed to a board tacked with family pictures and asked, "Have you ever seen *A River Runs Through It?*" We all nodded in unison like well-behaved school boys. (The movie was the reason most of us had tried fly-fishing in the first place.) Ron pointed to a slightly faded picture of a man in a nice suit standing in contemplative reverence, holding a Bible. "Well, that is my father there. He was a Methodist minister who taught me how to fish these waters around here. And my brother, well, he died when I was young. That movie is really close to the story of my life."

I felt a holy moment of invitation, as if this man was part of the answer I was searching for.

I left the table and gave myself the short tour around the few small rooms the cabin contained. On the old wooden-panel walls were old family pictures of mountaineering, rock-climbing, and fly-fishing adventures. They were all slowly fading to that color that let you know Ron had been at this awhile, that some of these adventures had been accomplished before I was born.

I would find out in time that Ron was not a member of our church. He had largely given up on organized religion during the days of McCarthyism. For reasons too complicated to fully explain here, his family had been forced away from its congregation because of his father's beliefs. But while Ron had left organized church, he had found something else—and rivers ran through it. He had been gathering his own congregation of men on the chilly waters of the Arkansas and South Platte rivers. The way Ron saw it, Jesus spent time with fishermen—and so did he. He also believed that fly-fishing in gorgeous river basins surrounded by brilliant wildflowers, dancing waters, and aspen-scented air set such a glorious scene that one couldn't help but meet Jesus there—fly rod in hand—simply by landing a rainbow trout. While most people were interested in the metaphor of Jesus and becoming a fisher of men, I think Ron was more interested in the actual experience of it. The sheer number of hours he spent on the river made it obvious that he was a dedicated, practicing believer in this method. Fishing had, in so many ways, become Ron's religion.

As I sat in that cabin for the first time with Ron, my disappointment in the simple lodging was replaced with a wonder at an older man and his buddies in the kitchen tying flies.

As I took it all in—the place, the man, what I had just been invited into—I felt as if this was the story I had been looking for. That night I slept in my sleeping bag on the concrete deck, breathing in the cool, fresh mountain air. I was ready to catch a fish.

In the morning we made the decision to split the group up and fish different rivers. I knew I was going with Ron. I was right next to him at the fly shop as he picked out a few extra flies. I asked him about his choices and picked out the same ones. I followed him as he waded out into the Big Thompson River, and he started teaching me the history of the place, the holes on the rivers, and where I needed to fish—just like a dad would.

After a while I started fishing just a little upriver of Ron. I moved up and down, in and out of riffles, casting the line and looking for trout where he had told me to cast. I watched as a black bear cub played in the water not a hundred yards in front of me. And then I caught a trout—a beautiful, shiny rainbow about ten inches long. The first thing I did was find Ron. He had seen me before I could even find him. I heard a loud whistle downriver followed by a less audible, "That's my boy!" The words sent chills down my spine.

We fished all day, but I would have sworn it was fifteen minutes. I was having so much fun, experiencing so much pleasure in the presence of these men as land and roaring water encircled me. I lost track of everything but my count: three. Three wonderful, sweet, delicious trout.

We gathered later that evening, all crammed together in that cabin. Ron singled me out from the group and said, "Nice fishing, partner. You are a good little fisherman. You were hitting it hard on the water today." And I tell you, it was as if God Himself was speaking to me. And then Ron's words: "We need to do this again." While I didn't know why, this fishing legend was pleased with me, enough to invite me to fly-fish again. And while we might have had a few differing opinions on church, I was ready and willing to be his disciple.

8

POWER

When we invented fight club, Tyler and I, neither of us had ever
been in a fight before. If you've never been in a fight, you wonder.
About getting hurt, about what you're capable of doing against
another man. I was the first guy Tyler ever felt safe enough to
ask … "I want you to do me a favor. I want you to hit me as hard
as you can." I didn't want to, but Tyler explained it all, about not
wanting to die without any scars, about being tired of watching
only professionals fight, and wanting to know more about himself.

Fight Club

From the moment my coworker John met me, with my eager, childish
face, soft suburban hands, and entitled spirit, it seemed his personal
mission was to break me like a school bully would the new kid. I
believe when a man has worked hard all his life, tasted firsthand the
misery of futility, and taken some hard licks, he has a special sense for

a man who has not. I was leaking blood in the water, an easy target for John's acute sense of smell.

John was one of the crew's hardest workers. He knew his way around paint and the details of jobs—and made sure others did too. He gave stern orders, which could be attributed to his previous career in the military. While handsome and square faced, a hard fight with alcohol and years of being in the sun had aged him considerably. His leathery face often appeared cold and hard, especially when he was talking with me. He was a man of few words and seemingly fewer feelings.

I have always been smaller than the average man, both in size and stature. As a teenager it seemed I was one of the last to hit puberty and emotionally mature. This held me back in athletics. I looked young and felt even younger. There was a certain smallness I felt from all of it. And when you feel small and you are male, you inevitably encounter the need to defend and protect yourself. John was the school bully I couldn't beat up or take down when I was a boy. He made all those insecurities resurface. And while I tried being the nice Christian guy, I secretly wanted to fight the dude (though I knew I was too small to actually do that and win).

Because John was my painting superior, I often had to take orders from him. While Carlos and Juan were more generous in their teaching and correction, John dramatically pointed out every mistake I made with a certain sense of pleasure. If I needed his help, he would scowl as if I was the greatest inconvenience he'd ever experienced. He also seemed to love to point out my problems—not just to me, but to the crew, as well, so I would look like a fool.

He rarely criticized me to my face. Most of the time I would hear him around the corner of the house as he said to Juan or Carlos, in a voice meant for me to hear, "He is taking forever on that trim over there." Or he would share with everyone how sloppy my caulk lines looked as I stood right next to him.

I wanted to destroy him.

What he was saying was often true. I was screwing up all the time. But my biggest problem was deeper than John. It was my shame of being so bad at my work. I felt that if I gave John an inch or showed weakness, he would pound me. So I started doing what I had done all my life—protecting myself, developing a thick skin, and feigning the attitude I didn't care about his comments or cut downs. Despite my fury, I usually took his verbal reprimands. I hated him, and yet I couldn't help but act like a puppy dog each time I saw him, hoping somehow he might validate me, or let off, or turn to help me with a gracious hand. I was begging for it. And I hated that, too.

Every work morning I prayed John would not show up or that he would be at another job site, or be drunk and still in bed. And each day, as I reported to the house, the steel-hard lines of his face would be there, waiting to greet me.

As I've mentioned, I was discovering that the nice little Christian boy I thought I was, was actually an angry, raging madman. But like everything in my life, I bottled it all up. It seemed that what stood between me and having a great work experience was this one man. He was blocking my path to moving forward and finding God at the job. If only John was removed, or just stayed out and drank and got fired from the job ... Can you see where this is going?

My coworker Jesse and I drove up to the house one morning and found John making a sexual gesture to us. I watched as Carlos laughed. That was it. I erupted. I jumped out of the car and got in his face. He shrunk back. All I remember next is carrying a thirty-two-foot ladder around with superhuman strength, tossing other metal ladders like bamboo sticks, and grunting as I slammed them on the ground, all the while staring down John. My inner rage had reared its ugly head. I locked gazes with John and saw fear in his eyes. And I felt something new. I felt powerful. I felt large. It was a great feeling.

The same thing happened at Home Depot a few months later. I was returning a cement mixer, and the man behind the rental counter told me it was still dirty. I had spent time cleaning it and hosing it off, and I knew that when I rented the thing, it was covered in cement. I explained all that to him, but he looked at me like an incompetent child who had never used a tool in his life. My explanations were greeted with stares and silence. I felt small. He then told me he was going to charge me a fee, and my anger erupted once again. No longer would men treat me this way. I questioned him, fired back a few lines to undercut his thoughts, and demanded to speak to his manager. I watched as this large man began to shrink back and become quiet. I let the manager know about his actions and walked out the door proud of my decision to stand up to a man.

It felt like a spiritual act, to speak my voice and not let men push me around. I had this amazing feeling inside. I had honored my inner voice in front of some very intimidating men I had always been scared of. I felt powerful.

It was probably wrong, but I loved both moments. I loved the thought that these men, while larger and older, might actually be scared of me. I felt like I had finally broken my leash.

◆

That week I went to see my counselor. I shared the stories of my newfound strength in action and assumed she would be thrilled. I imagined her smile and affirming words, maybe a, "Well done, Xan," or, "You are dealing well with men."

But she looked at me curiously and said, "So when you feel small, you make other men feel smaller?"

I just sat there. I wasn't feeling so great anymore. Not feeling so big. Were my new expressions not the answer? Had I just become the bully?

9

DESIRE

You want something but don't get it. You kill and covet, but
you cannot have what you want. You quarrel and fight. You
do not have, because you do not ask God. When you ask,
you do not receive, because you ask with wrong motives,
that you may spend what you get on your pleasures.

James 4:2–3

I always assumed that while I struggled with Internet pornography
before marriage, the struggle would end after getting married. For
months it did. I felt the freedom. Sex was great. But the old addiction
slowly crept back. I was in denial, but it was there, knocking at my
door.

It was all surfacing about the same time I was trying to understand my emotions—where my anger came from and how to really
feel. I was noticing how little I could show or feel emotions besides

anger. I realized it because of Jayne. She would look at me and say, "You look really tired." And I would think about it and realize I was tired. I had been tired all day. But somehow I never felt tired. I just pushed through, never stopped to check in with my own soul.

I was seeing that I did not know how to feel on my own. I needed my wife to tell me, or my counselor. I found myself talking to my wife a lot, going to her for comfort and help with processing my day. She's very empathetic, and I used that. I began to need her to tell me how I was feeling and to listen as I verbally unpacked the complexities of my day.

It was weird to see the correlation, but it seemed pornography was doing that for me too. I was using it to feel, to get all those emotions of pleasure, joy, or pain that were all twisted and locked up inside me.

It was a release.

While Jayne was at work one evening, I was sitting on the couch, bored. Soon I found myself looking at pornography on my computer again. I knew it was sinful. I knew it was horribly wrong—I was a married man and a Christian man—but I looked anyway. The porn led to a familiar habit: masturbation. Normally afterward I would bury myself in a nap or in Bible reading and repentance, exclaiming, "I will never do it again, Lord. I promise!"

But this time I went outside, up on the cliff a few feet above our house, and stared at the evening sunset down into the valley. I sat there with all my frustrations and shame. Then peace came over me. I realized I'd found what I was wanting inside my heart the whole time. I was looking for beauty and some quiet rest but had given myself a cheap substitute.

I also noticed how I was using my wife. At times I would ask her to comfort me, nurture me, and help me feel, to be more a mother than a wife. On a few occasions I had heard her say, "I can't be your mother." Looking back, I wonder if my mom should have modeled how it was to feel some of those emotions missing from my heart—hurt, pain, tears, and joy—and helped me give voice to my own emotions. But I don't have memories of crying on her shoulder or her comforting me over a breakup, or laughing a lot and enjoying things together. She seemed always strong, stable ... and stoic. In my family, emotions were not thought of as important things to worry about or evaluate. I don't know why, but we just never did that sort of thing.

My struggle with pornography seemed to stem from my need to feel and express my emotions. Even the images I searched for spoke to what I desired to feel at certain times. They almost described the varying needs of my heart: comfort, violence, or control. It was as if my sin was speaking to a deeper place in my heart that needed God—almost pointing to it.

Because my emotions went mostly unrecognized, they often welled up like a dammed river. After a few days, weeks, or months, even after fighting and much prayer, the dam would burst, rushing me downstream to pornography. I would immerse myself in the images and the feelings they would produce. Out West, I was slowly beginning to understand what I was looking for—and why. Please don't hear that as some excuse; I'm just trying to articulate an incredibly deep and shame-filled place.

I can remember working on my computer one day at a coffee shop when four women sat down a few feet in front of me: two beautiful mothers and two beautiful daughters my age. I was fighting the urge to look over and lust. I did my best to look away. This fight went on for a good twenty minutes. I couldn't even concentrate enough to continue typing. Finally I stopped trying and took out my journal. I decided to try and write out what I wanted, a full expression of the moment.

I wrote this:

> I want these four women to want me, to not be able to take their eyes off me. And then for them to reach for me and hold me, just hold me … I'm younger, much younger …

I stopped, looked at the words I wrote, and asked God, *What is this desire really about? What is really behind this coffee-shop fantasy?*

The answers came: *Xan, you want to be loved. You want to be admired and nurtured. Held. Cared for. And loved.*

All of a sudden I didn't feel like something disgusting. I had honored my desire instead of just bouncing my eyes. And instead of feeling shame, I saw a little boy inside who needed to be held, nurtured. I just wanted to be loved by someone—probably God. That was it.

I had been turning every other place to find that.

What if the deeper desire—deeper than pornography—was for God? What if He was speaking to me all that time and I just never honored the true desire behind it all? I stopped right there in the coffee shop and prayed: *Lord, I need mercy. Would You be that nurturing part that I somehow need inside? Maybe even the mother I am in search of.* I felt like, right then, something significant happened in my heart. I had let God in it. I had emotions and asked God to meet me in them. My struggle with pornography did not just vanish, but I was starting to get in touch with something deep within—a longing that had to do with my heart and my need for a strong, tender, nurturing, feminine part of God I had no idea I so deeply needed.

10

ENTITLEMENT

For young men who have graduated from privileged colleges, or
who have been lifted upward by the expensive entitlement culture,
their soul life often begins with this basement work in the kitchen.

Robert Bly, *Iron John*

I was beginning to settle into the rhythm of painting: the morning
drudgery, the rise for lunch, the five o'clock whistle. To be honest, I
thought the drawn-out monotony of a job like that would kill me.
There was plenty to complain and be frustrated about, but I was still
alive.

It was during one of those ordinary days that the crew—Carlos,
Juan Carlos, Jack, John, Jesse, and I—squeezed together at a table,
munching on burritos after prepping a house. As I looked around,
it was obvious just how much we stood out. In fact white men in
white collars and business suits surrounded us. It felt like being in

Brentwood again—but on the other side. I was covered in paint and rather dirty. I couldn't help but start to feel my position as a laborer. I stared at their nice suits, then looked back at my caulk-stained pants.

The table of guys reminded me of myself, my roots and what I had left in Nashville—including the promise of the business world. I felt like I was staring at what I could have been. Or what I should be. I felt horrible thinking it, but I had this desperate urge to walk over to their table and say, "Hey, I am one of you. It's not what it looks like. Let me sit down here with you."

It was the first time I publicly felt where I was and who I was with. And I was embarrassed.

I never knew how much I had grounded myself in that identity, as a well-to-do, upper-class, educated guy, until I left it—and really not until that lunch. I guess that's why all the collared Ralph Lauren Polo shirts with that signature horse and my new Orvis gear meant so much to me: They were part of an image, one that I still somehow felt was required to maintain. But there I was, stripped of it with no way to get the white-collared men to like me. I was wearing working clothes of a different class. I felt like a nobody, a laborer on a crew with a bunch of rough, working-class men. I was eating a burrito while sandwiched between two worlds.

It happened in other places too. I would walk into a mall or a restaurant in my grubby work clothes after a long day's work, and I swear people would look at me differently. I have to admit it probably had more to do with my perception and insecurities than anything. But whether it was external or internal, there was a shift, and I noticed it.

I felt this subtle need to differentiate myself, to let my coworkers know there was more to me. I would check my cell phone e-mail for messages about important matters or take a lunch break without the crew at times, or drop in some story to let the crew know I was a writer, or tell them about my previous life in Brentwood. And while no one said anything to my face, I could feel the separation. I wasn't as close as the other men. They knew I thought I was above them—despite being below them in skill and expertise.

I was coming to see that my attitude had everything to do with the word *entitlement*. I felt I deserved something more, and I saw myself as better than the men around me. Painting was just a job for a short season of my life; then I would get to more important things in business or ministry. These men might still be painting years from now, but not me—I had a ticket out. And in some ways I was ready to cash in and get out.

I had spent a lot of my life judging people in the position I found myself in. I used to look at a van with ladders on top, filled with Latinos, driving through my hometown of Brentwood and make assumptions and judgments about the men inside.

But here I was, really getting to know these men, and I liked them. Juan Carlos drove a van and was a good man who could make me laugh. I admired him for his work ethic and his working another job on the weekends to support his immediately family members, who lived with him, and his extended family members, who lived in Mexico. It was the same with Carlos; he was teaching me both about his Latino culture and how to actually paint and roll walls from the kindness of the heart. All day we would listen to Latino channels on the radio, one mariachi song after another. Carlos would translate the words into English as I tried to figure out how each love song didn't say the same thing as the others. We spent many long days talking about immigration and the day's news. I truly enjoyed him and appreciated his company. He even taught me how to dance reggaeton, a combination of Latin and techno, at a coworker's party. These men were becoming my friends.

And that is why my lunch hour that day was so horribly confusing. I was coming to really respect this table of men, yet I was still embarrassed to associate myself with them at times. Embarrassed of what I looked like and smelled like and seemed like. The shift was occurring, only at a tortoise's pace.

11

MOTHER

We cannot but pity the boy who has never fired a gun.

Henry David Thoreau

We are an entire generation raised by women. I'm wondering
if another woman is really the answer we need.

Fight Club

If I was going to hunt, I was going to need a gun.

I began the search for a high-caliber, bolt-action rifle with a
mounted scope. As I stared into the glass cases of firearms, I would
ask the men to take them out so I could feel the grain of the wood
stock and look down the shiny metal barrel. I would grab the rifle
and try to hold it as if I had some sense of what I was doing. I always
worried that the men behind the counter would look at me and tell
me I wasn't eligible to buy one. Maybe they would laugh at me—*You?*

A gun?—like I was too young. Or too small. Not responsible enough or qualified to bear arms.

And then the questions: Could I handle it? Was I really ready? Would I end up shooting myself? What would my mom think?

I first shot a gun in Boy Scouts. As a kid I attended Boxwood Summer Camp for an entire week of campfires, crafts, and guns. It was the first time I had ever fired a small rifle—and I did it with a big smile on my face. Being a domesticated kid from the suburbs, where jumping out of a minivan and suffering a wild kick in the shin at a soccer game topped the list of most-dangerous activities, I was in love with the thought of a bullet strategically surging through a paper target at my command. I kept wondering why the camp folks let us shoot them; they seemed so dangerous. But I spent every free second at the shooting range, firing rounds like I was training for war. I had never felt such power.

When I arrived home from scout camp, I worked on my parents, convincing them I needed a small rifle. It was a nearly impossible task. They explained that there was not enough room in our backyard for a real rifle. Besides, they said, it was impractical and too dangerous. The resulting compromise was a BB gun that could barely make a dent in a soda can. Even so, my parents felt it was too powerful a weapon for me to keep in my possession, so it stayed under their bed and close to my mother's side for safekeeping. I always had to ask to use it. There was something about my mother holding the key to exploration and danger—something that bothered me a bit.

Guns are a controversial and fiery topic in America, in part because the modern suburban male has no real need for weapons. But for centuries that was not the case. As Robert Bly wrote, "We know that for hundreds of thousands of years men have admired each other, and been admired by women, in particular for their activity. Men and women alike once called on men to pierce dangerous places, carry handfuls of courage to the waterfalls, dust the tails of the wild boars. All knew that if men did that well the women and children could sleep safely."[10]

A man was required to use his physical strength and skill to survive and protect his family. But as technology progressed, many of man's primitive symbols became obsolete and vanished from everyday use. Powerful weapons like axes, swords, bows and arrows, and guns, used for obtaining meat, were replaced with modern farming methods and stockpiled grocery stores. Men didn't need to rise and defend their homes; the police were called to do that. And if the country was at war, well, that's what all those paid soldiers are for. What had constituted man's identity—carrying home the meat, defending his home and family—had mostly been contracted out. We outsourced much of what man had been known to be good for.

For the last twenty years the answer to Columbine and other incidents of school violence has often been, "Ban the guns. They're too dangerous." But the problem is deeper than that. Truth is, a boy needs power. He will find it in some form, good or bad. I think he needs an older man to show him how to wield that power and strength for good. The problem is no one is initiating boys into power wielding.

God's creation of man and woman in the garden has very intentional, symbolic meaning. Man was designed with a bit larger frame, wider shoulders, fuller muscles, and a deeper voice. It is a touchy subject in many places—you don't want to get labeled sexist or oversell it—but God designed us intentionally. Man was given a penis, which could be seen as a symbol of virility; it was meant to rise up, penetrate, and protrude. Man is about movement and strength. A woman's body was shaped more tenderly, with great vulnerability; it's open and inviting. You can see similar traits in the sperm and egg: The sperm moves to enter the egg, and the egg receives the sperm. God reveals the heart of man and woman through even these symbols. It seems that we have lost all symbols of masculinity. It's as if they've all disappeared but the one we could not lose: the one that's still attached.

One wealthy and God-fearing friend confessed to spending hours online looking at guns. He has every gun he needs for hunting, but he wants more. We could write these off as mere props, stuff with which to play cowboys and Indians. But it's deeper than that, as if our hearts are crying out for something—as if the symbols themselves are pointing to need, origin, and longing.

I didn't see it initially, but when it came time to buy this rifle, I felt it necessary to call my parents and ask for it as a gift. It was partly because I was broke and Christmas was coming, but I also believe I was looking for my mom's approval. I needed to see if she would grant me permission, say it was okay to have one now that I was an adult. In some sense I was calling to see if I could finally get the gun out from under her bed and use it again.

The conversation went like this:

> Hey, I think I know what I would love for you guys
> to consider for a Christmas gift this year.
>
> Oh, great. What is that?
>
> A rifle.
>
> (Silence. More silence.) … What? You aren't going
> to kill Bambi, are you?

I was so embarrassed. I was a grown man, married with a mortgage, and by all means past the leaving and cleaving stage. Some men my age had fought in wars—flown jets, driven tanks, and sacrificed their lives for their country. And here I was, practically heading back to my mother's side of the bed, and requesting permission like a little child.

I really don't think I am alone in this. It seems that over the years, one of the greatest issues facing America is mothers' over-nurturing of their sons.

My friend and counselor, Sam Jolman, says there is a process a boy needs to go through to step into manhood. It goes from mother to father to God. A boy receives his mother's nurturing—her milk, her care, and tenderness. But as a boy grows and his body changes to reflect this, there is a transition that needs to occur. His father must lead him away from the nurturing, care, and protection into masculinity, risk, and his own power and strength. But there is a tension between mom and dad. Mom's maternal instinct wants to hold the boy as a child, but Dad is to draw the boy out of the mother's arms. Masculinity bestows masculinity.

Richard Rohr explains in *Adam's Return* that for the aboriginal culture, the ax was a symbol of manhood. It was a powerful tool that allowed aborigines to farm, hunt, chop down trees, and provide for their village. The aboriginal men and warriors understood that a boy needed to learn how to wield his weapon. He was not handed one as a child. He did not make one on his own or purchase one. It was only given to him when he was ready for it. During this ceremony men would take him out to the place of the stone ax, where he was to make his ax from the stone only after he had been initiated by the men. They believed a boy was not ready for power—and this ax—until he had the inner strength to wield it. He had to prove that. When the boy returned to the village with his ax, it was a sign to the community the boy had become a man.[11]

As we lost our symbols, we also lost the fathers. With fathers having nothing to initiate us into, we were left to our mothers and their inner world. Close to their domestication and care. We might call these sorts of guys momma's boys. Metrosexuals. Gentlemen. Girly men. Child-men. All these terms we use for boys who have become over-bonded to their mothers and have had few male influences. Rohr writes, "Unless a young male is shown real power through a community of wise elders, he will always seek false power and likely will spend much of his life seeking prestige, perks, and possessions."[12]

Is it surprising that without authentic masculine symbols, and with no men to guide us, our culture's symbol of masculinity is women? We stayed close to the world of women because it was all we knew. Without men to lead us, and with our mothers still holding the key to our power, we looked for women to validate us. They appeared to hold the key to manhood.

I saw this in my need for pornography. After I married I assumed it would just go away. But it didn't. Once again I found myself in secrets, searching to feel something that I could not understand—as if the naked woman held that power. I had been using pornography since I was a young boy. I gave my body to fantasy to, in some sense, validate me and make me feel powerful. Instead of looking for other forms of true strength, I initiated myself with a fantasy woman.

My search for a beautiful woman to have on my arm continued in college. The search dominates our culture today. A man's woman becomes his trophy, his validation as a man.

Looking back on my journey, I am not sure if I was ever told by men that I should search for inner strength. Or that there is great power to be wielded with the new spirit of Christ in me. For the most part it was about ridding myself of my sin, and I think I just interpreted that whatever was inside of me, even the new heart given to me in Christ, needed to be watched like a boy in time-out—not unleashed or empowered.

Richard Rohr says that when a man does not feel power internally, when he does not walk free and full as a man in Christ, he begins to attach to things that have it.[13] External things. A sports team. Money. A vehicle. Success. A girl. Even a country. We look for things that contain power because we do not feel powerful. We find the next best thing, and we cling to it. It seems marketers push on men products that promise to give man back their symbols. Harleys promise freedom and the roar and rush of joy. Ford Mustangs promise serious horsepower. A cigar will bring back rest and influence; a beer will bring us the girls and the party we're searching for.

Head to a magazine rack and see them showcased.

As I walked through Walmart one day it all made sense. Remember the aborigines' symbol of masculinity? An ax. Well there it was, Axe: a line of body and hair products created specifically for young men. The brand's slogan? "Get girl-approved hair" … as if attaining a woman's validation is the ultimate goal. I thought back to the Axe commercials I'd seen with sexy girls flinging themselves on guys who had doused their bodies in cologne. Dudes who put on Axe were rewarded with erotic experiences. When I visited the Axe Web site the other day, it featured a bikni-clad model with dark, ruffled hair, bent over in the middle of the forest. The tagline? "Get more."

Axe's Web site states, "Our products are based on the consumer insight that guys groom to get the girl." The great symbol of true masculine power today—Axe. The marketing ploy: Women hold the power to manhood. Nothing is required of me. Just buy it and spray it on.

I must confess, I don't think a gun is the answer—not for every man. But at the time, a gun was a tool I could use to find power and validation outside of a woman—and in a man's world. It was my ax. With it I was moving toward the masculine, toward something I could put my hands on that was not a woman or my own body. It was powerful. Store bought, yes. But it was moving me into a new place.

A few weeks later I drove to a public shooting range with my shiny new rifle—a Christmas present from my parents. I showed up on my own. I sat down on the metal bench, pulled out the massive bullets, and began to load the rifle one bullet at a time.

I sat there holding a loaded weapon. I knew it was time to put my shoulder against the rifle and squeeze the trigger. But I was frozen with the fear that I might have screwed something up. What if I had bought the wrong ammo or not loaded them in the rifle correctly? Would I be okay? The gun felt so much more powerful than me. Would it backfire? Shoot the other direction and kill me? I was paralyzed with this horrible fear that I was mishandling it. Here I was with a real gun, and my greatest fear was that I could not properly handle it. Looking back, I think I needed a community of men to surround me, to give me some direction and reassure me.

I took a breath and inched into the gun, looking down the scope to my paper target a hundred yards away, bracing my shoulder to the stock of the gun. Then I closed my eyes and squeezed the trigger. I felt a bang. The force of the rifle kicked back like a jackhammer, slamming the scope right into my eye. I had just fired my rifle. And while I had not braced myself correctly, and there was no bullet on the paper, my eye was stinging to prove it.

12

MOSES

The lowliness happens particularly to men
who are initially high, lucky, elevated.

Robert Bly, *Iron John*

As I read through Scripture, I noticed a pattern of God taking
men from privileged, entitled positions and leading them out to a
desert—or among caves, or into a prison, or into the belly of a fish—
to teach them something they couldn't have learned in their previous
positions. Abraham is asked to go to a land and a country he knows
not of, leaving all his wealth. Job, also a blessed man, is stripped
of everything—family, possessions, lifestyle—all of his entitlements.
David is anointed as God's chosen leader before being forced to go on
the run from Saul for years, away from the people he is called by God
to rule. Even Joseph goes from a cherished and beloved son to being
placed into a pit by his brothers, sold into slavery, and imprisoned

by Potiphar's wife for no fault of his own. It seemed that when God wanted to use a man, He had to take him to a place he didn't want to go to in order to prepare him.

There might be no greater picture of this than Moses.

Americans often think of the U.S. as the lone superpower. But long before us, before Europe's Renaissance, before the magnificence of Rome, the wisdom of the Greek and Persians, and even the vastness of Babylon, Egypt was a superpower as well, with gold, riches, and incalculable dominance throughout the known world. With its super-power status came plenty of development and building projects. Egypt needed workers, and this task rested primarily on the backs of the Israelites, whom God had led into Egypt to become slaves.

While the Israelites were forced into slave labor, making clay bricks from mud and straw, God was blessing their families with lots of babies. They were becoming so large in number that they threatened the security of the Egyptians. In the interest of Egypt, Pharaoh decided to kill all the new babies in fear that their overpopulation might eventually lead to a rebellion. It was during this decree that Moses was born. If he were discovered, he would be killed.

As any good mother would have, Moses' mother devised a plan that, along with God's providential rescue of this young boy, would give him a better life. She put him in a rigged-up, floating basket and sent him down the river to the Pharaoh's daughter, who saw the baby and took Moses in as one of her own.

Moses was adopted and raised like a son of the pharaoh. He grew up in the presence of the greatest educators. The Scriptures make this clear: Acts 7:22 says, "Moses was instructed in all the wisdom of the

Egyptians and was powerful in speech and action." He didn't just look good; he was confident, bold, and a growing leader.

And for the next forty years, while his people faced adversity and suffering, slaving away in the hot sun and making bricks, Moses was raised in the cool of the courtyards with a private education and tutors. He dined with queens and kings and wore some really fancy Egyptian clothes. One day he decided to stroll through the working area to see his people. Exodus 2:11 says he "watched them at their hard labor." He was a pampered Egyptian dandy who had yet to feel any of their pain and suffering. And it showed.

"He saw an Egyptian beating a Hebrew, one of his own people. Glancing this way and that and seeing no one, he killed the Egyptian and hid him in the sand" (Ex. 2:11–12). Acts 7:25 goes on to say, "*Moses thought that his own people would realize that God was using him to rescue them, but they did not.*" Is this making more sense? He had a messiah complex. He thought the people would look up to him, but they didn't—not all those blue-collar workers baking in the sun. The following day an Israelite who heard of the murder spoke to Moses and said, "Who made you ruler and judge over us?" (Ex. 2:14). Or in other words, "You gold-spoon-living pretty boy!"

Moses thought he was ready to lead, maybe even impress his fellow Israelites with his actions. But no respect was given to this privileged man with soft skin and expensive clothes. It was confusing to Moses. He had all the gifts and power, the influence, the training. I hadn't ever read the story that way before, but I could see there was something God wanted to teach Moses, something missing in his story—mainly because it was missing in mine, too.

Moses had never experienced slavery, wilderness, sweat, bondage, suffering, or abandonment by God. He never had to work, never had to feel brokenness or loss of identity. So God separates him from his education, his privilege, his title, and all his fancy clothes. Moses is driven into the wilderness as an outlaw, to a barren land where his Egyptian upbringing is of no significance. It's all gone in an instant.

It is a shocking experience going from privilege to nothing. Robert Bly explains it like this: "One day he is in college, being fed and housed—often on someone else's money—protected by brick walls men long dead have built, and the next day he is homeless, walking the streets, looking for some way to get a meal and a bed."[14]

As I began to listen to other young men, the same theme reappeared: young Christian college leaders with great promise who saw themselves as great men. Their parents had consistently told them they could achieve their dreams. They knew Scripture and had received the knowledge and teaching to carry it out. The Christian campus leaders exalted them for their gifts, praised them for their talents. But the truth is we are just a bunch of Moseses before the wilderness and the forty years. We were given everything, which is partially a good thing because we were provided for, but we were never told there are other seasons to walk in—growing seasons. We had not walked through much suffering or had many real-world experiences, never been through a war or a depression. Never had to ask God for our next meal or shelter over our head. We understand the world mostly from inside the air-conditioned temple courts like Moses. And like him, we think we are ready to lead.

Moses had three seasons of his life: forty years of privilege and entitlement, forty years of abandonment and wilderness, and forty years of leading God's people.

It seems God takes men to this wilderness and foreign place to sober them up and prepare them. Bly writes, "The lowliness happens particularly to men who are initially high, lucky, elevated … Our ego doesn't want to do it and even if we drop, the ego doesn't want to see it."[15] It seemed God did this particularly to those who had lived a life of extra privilege. Part of my problem was that I wasn't searching for it, and I didn't have people explaining this as a necessary season to go through.

I think this is why Eugene Peterson said, "Our spiritual life begins—seriously begins—when we get a job and go to work."[16] There was a place I needed to go that I could not understand, nor did I really have people explaining to me. My life, and the lives of so many of American's young men, reflects that of Moses. We are educated. Promoted. Seen as the gifts of the next generation. Empowered. Blessed. Given great things beyond the previous generation. It seems so good, so right. And we love it. But then we struggle and fail to launch into adulthood, and people ask, "What happened? Why?"

I thought I was the next thing, that God needed me to lead.

I think my blue-collar work was part of that experience I needed to sober me up. My boss, Mike, needed me to show up at 8 a.m. and caulk lines and paint. That is all. It was humbling and hard. The job required my physical labor. All those other things I had been given, my "talents," didn't matter here. My education didn't mean anything.

Not my words or way of explaining things. Or charm. Nothing. Working that job went against everything I thought of myself, of what I was worth and what I should be doing.

But I think God was taking me to a place I did not want to go, into pain, my story, and away from the privilege of Brentwood and my own ideas of finding God in a new way. I was lured out to Colorado with grand visions of finding the Almighty while scaling mountains, but to truly find Him, I actually had to descend. Richard Rohr explains it as going down to your cross into suffering and pain, much like Jesus chose on His cross.[17] Unless you go there, you can't understand the hope of the resurrection. Jesus said, "If anyone would come after me, he must deny himself and take up his cross and follow me" (Mark 8:34). While I had lived the first part of my life as the privileged son of Brentwood in the courts, those days were gone.

Long gone.

13

$8

No country can sustain, in idleness, more than a small percentage of its numbers. The great majority must labor at something productive.

Abraham Lincoln

The sleep of a laborer is sweet, whether he eats little or much, but the abundance of a rich man permits him no sleep.

Ecclesiastes 5:12

I was making eight dollars an hour to paint. I had made more than eight dollars an hour when I was an immature teen mowing yards in my neighborhood. I was now an adult, a private school- and college-educated man, twenty-seven years of age, making a measly eight dollars an hour. There were many tough things about the job, but this was the worst. It was completely contrary to the idea of working smarter, not harder, and moving upward, not downward.

And it was the opposite of everything I had tried to make of myself and where I thought I would be at this stage in life. I was making less than Carlos, Juan Carlos, Juan, John, and on equal pay with Jack, who was fifteen and had dropped out of high school. And even he was a better painter than me (though I did not want to admit that).

I kept feeling like I was worth more. Deserved more pay. The numbers played over and over in my head. It was ludicrous. I hated hearing how much I was making for the boss each day. To work for so little, almost peanuts, knowing what I thought I was worth, and even aware I was being billed out at forty dollars an hour to clients to do the labor. I wanted to grab the paint crew and start a revolt. We could start our own company and cut out our boss from all the loot. The number eight weaved in and out of my head so many times in a day that sometimes I thought it would make me crazy. I felt like a prisoner. Prisoner number eight.

I grew up believing money was going to come my way. It would fall off a tree and just roll on the ground until it found me. I was expectant. I wasn't a super-greedy, money-grubbing kid, but I grew up in an upper-class lifestyle. My parents had paid for most things, and I had learned money would find a way to me. It always had. It was never a worry. But then I graduated, and suddenly it stopped. They cut me off. I was on my own.

When I had made forty-five dollars a lawn in high school, my expenses were two dollars for gas, leaving forty-three dollars of net profit. I could use it on anything I wanted. But having my own bills to pay, I was now finding that each month I was starting out in the negative.

From a white-collar perspective that sees everything in annual salaries and cycles, making eight dollars an hour was horribly depressing. A corporate suit might say, "I make six figures," or, "I make $200,000 a year"— a collective amount gathered over a period of hundreds of days and hundreds of hours. That same corporate suit might say, "I saved the corporation $10,000 a year." He does not say, "I saved the company four dollars an hour." He multiplies the savings over the entire year, then reports the large number. I was trained to think the same way, to take all the numbers and extend them until they look even larger, because larger numbers make you feel powerful. The larger the numbers, the more important you are.

While white collars dealt with multiplication, I was learning that blue collars dealt with division. You took all these big numbers that the people used and divided them to understand what they really amounted to on a more practical level. Everything had to be divided from the rich man's terms of use, broken into more tangible figures to understand what it cost by the hour. There was not a salary here. I simply made eight dollars an hour. A single digit. No added zeroes to the end of it. No multiplying. For a man working for an hourly wage, every minute counts as money made or lost. And when you are working a job that takes so much out of you, I believe you need to know what it breaks down to, by the hour, and even the minute. I was worth just over a dime and three pennies per minute to be exact. I am not going to lie: I had never thought this way.

It all started making sense to me why they showed monthly pay-ments on the Home Shopping Network. A nice fruit juicer could be bought for three easy payments of twenty-nine dollars and ninety-nine cents. Even a stainless steel gas grill at Home Depot was broken down into low monthly payments of nineteen dollars a month for others who bought things in that fashion. And then for those who needed the monthly figures divided down even further, Rent-a-Center offers televisions for eleven dollars a week.

While I had never understood this concept and saw it as a rip-off, a terrible scheme to rob the poor, when you make eight dollars an hour, you starting thinking that a television set for eleven dollars a week is not a bad deal. And it is about all you can afford.

My new math, which had turned to division, looked something like this:

> *$160 gas and electric bill/$8 an hour=20 hours of work*
> *to pay our gas and electric bill*
> *$104 cell phone bill/$8 an hour=13 hours of work to pay*
> *our phone bill*
> *$40 steak dinner at Texas Roadhouse with Jayne/$8 an*
> *hour=5 hours of work to enjoy some meat*

I started dividing the price of everything. A half hour of work for every Starbucks drink, four hours of work every month to have Internet service on my phone, five hours for a month of cable television, or fifteen hours for that Osprey backpack I still wanted.

It was terribly depressing. Every day I spent my lunch break frustrated because I was not making money and in fact losing it. If I spent six dollars on lunch at Subway it would mean that I needed to work forty minutes when I got back to the job site to cover the cost of that meal. If I chose to eat out, that was an hour and a half of my day I spent working for nothing. Depressing again.

The painting job came along right on time because the money I had earned from the sale of the house in Knoxville had vanished. For the past few months I had been using my credit card to avoid the pain of not having money and not knowing what to do. I would swipe it a few times here, a few more there. The minimum payment on our $2,500 credit card balance was $85 a month. This was even more depressing. I could work an entire day at the job and still not make enough to pay the minimum payment on our credit card bill.

I complained, cussed, argued, kicked, and fought. What I did not know at the time was that all this hard work and hourly waging was really giving me a tangible perspective on money—one I didn't receive during my youth. The only way to receive this valuable lesson was the hard way. I was looking at goods and products, even gear, based on how much it took to work with my own sweat. Because my parents paid all of my bills in college, I had no real understanding of what things cost. Until that number eight came around. It was bringing about a real humbling reality of my life.

I used a Dave Ramsey budget and decided to put together the numbers, plugging in the bills and putting money where it needed to go. Entering in expenses like oil changes, insurance, and our credit cards. By the time I was done, I had spent all the money Jayne and I were going to make during the next month before we had even made it. No money for Starbucks, a book on eBay, or additional gear. It was probably one of the most depressing moments of my life. I wanted to shoot myself. I showed the budget to my wife, and the first thing she said was, "We have that much debt on credit cards?" She was shocked. I hadn't told her because I was too ashamed. Controlling the bills had been my way of covering it up.

I was slowly coming to understand the real value of work through painting—one hour at a time. The number I despised was the number I needed: my lucky number eight.

14

LADDER

All history has been a history of class struggles between
dominated classes at various stages of social development.

Friedrich Engels

It was about 6 p.m. on a Friday night.

We were working late, finishing a full interior repaint of a very
expensive home in a posh part of Colorado Springs. It reminded me
a lot of my boyhood house in Brentwood. It had taken the whole
crew the entire week to complete, and we were pushing to finish
because the moving van was arriving that weekend.

I was doing my final touch-ups in the foyer up on a ladder above
the glass front entryway, about eighteen feet in the air, when the
homeowner, the husband of the wife we had been working with all
week, came in directly underneath me. He was impeccably dressed
in a pressed wool suit, and from what the boss had explained earlier

that week, he had moved his family here for a job with a financial company. He greeted his wife and then began his self-guided tour around the house.

I watched as he walked by Carlos and Juan Carlos, who were finishing the trim right in front of the staircase. Then Jack and John, who were in the dining area touching up some lines. Then the rest of the crew. The man passed by each of the painters, but no one offered words; everyone put his head down and kept working. The place turned silent. I kept pretending I was painting as I followed his path, mesmerized at the silence, realizing I was experiencing something meaningful and confusing.

I knew my crew didn't respect white-collar men in business suits. They saw white-collar work as easy work. To them real work required physical exertion. Rich people got out of working hard by using their brains instead of sweat and muscle. The pride of a blue-collar man was that he worked harder than guys like the new owner of this house.

But I could see the crew's self-esteem deflate the moment this man walked in his house. I had asked one of the guys earlier in the week if through some hard work and advancement they could see themselves in a similar home one day. The guy looked at me and laughed, saying, "A guy like me? Come on, I'm a laborer. I never graduated high school. I won't ever get to live in a house like this."

There was a sense of working for someone else's wealth, for "the man." I could see the shame they held in their faces. This man in his suit was the true image of masculinity, and they were merely his slaves. He was the boss, and they were his hired workers. They weren't smart enough; they would never able to hold a job like his. In their eyes he was the real man.

It was the same for the man in the suit. There was a pride in him, too, a pride I could identify with. He worked smarter, not harder. He used his intellect, which was given great respect in his job and our culture. His paycheck and the size of this house proved it. He knew his time was far too valuable to spend doing the mindless work other men could complete—work he couldn't do, work that maybe even seemed below him.

But despite the enormous amount of money he made and the size of his stock portfolio, he was walking into a house of men who had spent a week with his wife while working on his house. All he really did was sign the check. This had to be very awkward for him. And while he looked unfazed by the experience, his quietness and lowered head made it appear as if he felt tremendous shame—shame I could relate to.

I had heard similar things from friends. One guy who works in an office and on the phone most of the day shared in a confession, "I have soft hands. I want calloused hands." Another man who drives by men working construction at 7 a.m. while on his way to his office drools at the physicality of their work.

I had never felt such separation, but I saw it all so clearly up on that ladder, slightly removed from it all. For the first time I saw both sides. It made sense why neither of these men could easily connect, look each other in the eye, and smile. It hit me that day how much of our world was divided. How life experiences, our backgrounds and ways of growing up, unfortunately split us often into two categories: rich and poor, owners and slaves, Jews and Samaritans, peasants and nobles, kings and servants. The working class and ruling class. First class and second class. Corporate and union. White collar and blue collar. Even our politics often seem divided on those lines. The Democrat for the working class, and Republican for the wealthy. I had never seen it until God put me on this crew and gave me some perspective on this ladder to watch it all clash.

It seemed that each man had a part of true masculinity, but not the whole. There was a need for both physical and mental labor. And yet somehow it all got separated out. You were either one or the other.

But maybe we needed each other. Maybe there was something Carlos could teach this man that he really needed. And maybe this man in a suit had something to teach Carlos as well. But somehow, with all our collected pride and all the shame most of us didn't want to confess, we held ourselves back. We stuck in our corners and let it play out.

It was almost as if, while they would have never admitted it, each admired the other guy, the other class, the other side. That if we could have taken away all the shame and pride, instead of silence, the men would be slapping each other on the back, congratulating each other, praising each other for the type of work he did, asking for advice and tips. The homeowner would rip off his sports jacket and pick up a paintbrush as he watched Carlos and Juan Carlos teach him how to cut a line. Following that, the homeowner would lead a session on investing in stock options while the paint crew sat on buckets, taking notes.

It made me wonder if we were all hiding in fear, deeply afraid of being exposed for the men we were not. The truth was, white collar or blue collar, rich or poor, none of us felt like we measured up.

15

OIL

I didn't even know how to replace my own car muffler.
When I came to own a house, I wasted money on plumbers
to fix leaky faucets and electricians to repair broken light
switches … Even if he could have afforded it, my father
would never have ceded so much mastery of his world
over to hired hands. But I had done what young men in
America are supposed to do. I had risen in society.

Walt Harrington, *Everlasting Stream*

My past years of oil changes looked like this:

First minute: Give a guy my keys. Tell him my phone number.

Second through thirteenth minute: Walk over to their waiting room. Drink some cheap coffee from a tiny cup. Sit in a dirty metal chair from the '80s. Read *Motor Trend* magazine from the '90s while *The Jerry Springer Show* is on television.

Fourteenth minute: Rise up at the call of "Hood." Give the person my credit card for a thirty-five-dollar charge. Get in my car and drive away.

I never knew how easy it was to change the oil until Earl, Cory's dad, took me through it. He unscrewed the oil plug, drained the oil, changed the filter, and added more oil, then screwed it all back in place. It seemed so simple, so elementary school. It was so easy it was embarrassing. I decided that instead of paying someone to turn a few knobs, I would do it myself.

I bought a jack, some jack stands, the oil filter, and oil.

Here is how it looked this time in my garage:

First minute: Put the jack under my car. Begin to jack.

Third minute: Realize I am jacking up the wrong place. Shoot, there is a dent forming.

Fifth minute: Un-jack it. Jack under where the real frame is, put the jack stand under it, and do it on the other side while feeling good because I learned my lesson on the other side. Got this one right on the first try. Yes.

Ninth minute: Get under the hood. But I realize I'm not sure if I put the parking break on. I go check it. I feel relieved. I did.

Eleventh minute: Go back under the car. Lay there in search of the oil screw while realizing I could be a pancake if my jack stands don't hold. I unscrew the oil screw; the oil rushes out like black, liquid gold. Rush to put the oil pan under it; the oil is spilling out, dripping all over my hand. I forgot a towel. Leave to find one.

Thirteenth minute: Wait for the oil to drain.

Nineteenth minute: I try to unscrew the oil filter. But I can't by hand. I call Cory, who says I am doing it right. I go back under. But can't force the thing off. I start whacking my plastic wrench against the filter. Whack it a bit more. Cuss. Realize I need a different tool. I bought the wrong thing. Why did I choose plastic?

Twenty-ninth minute: So I drive down the road to Ace Hardware. Find a metal one. Wait, there are three sizes to pick from. Which size is mine? I forgot to bring the filter, so I just guess it might be the middle wrench. Not sure. I gamble, hoping it's right.

Fifty-ninth minute: Get back to my house, check the filter. I guessed right. Celebrate for a second. Go under the car, start pulling with my new tool. Pull. And pull. Filter is still not moving. I look up and realize the circle has been dented so much it has now become a square. I yank harder and realize my last whack punctured a hole in the oil filter. Oil is starting to spill out. It's getting all over me—including my face. I rush to put the oil pan under. Wipe myself off and go back for round eight and nine of the pulling. Still wondering if I am screwing it off in the right direction.

Sixty-seventh minute: The round-turned-square can has now become a carved-out pumpkin with a bunch of holes. I yank the thing, and it finally begins to slide. I yank more. Celebrate more. Start taking it off. Feeling like a mechanic.

Seventy-sixth minute: Put on the new oil filter. Ratchet the plug back in. I get out my oil. Unscrew the engine cap that says 5W-30. Oh wait, the can I bought says 10W-30. Another mistake. I say, "Screw it. It's going in. I am not going back to the store. It's only five numbers off anyway." Oil is oil, right? Sure. I fill it up, test the line. Almost done. Feeling like Dale Earnhardt's mechanic.

Eighty-second minute: I take the jack to the frame, remove both jack stands, and drop the hood. Put away my jack stands and walk in my house. I am a man.

Eighty-ninth minute: Wait. I realize I never pulled out the pan or tools under the car. Go back outside and remove them from underneath. Put the tools away.

I just changed the oil. And I swear to you, I felt like I just won the lottery or something.

I think what surprised me most is that I finished it. To think I had beaten myself up with shame and self-contempt and hatred along the way for being an idiot. Normally when I first make a mistake I think, *You idiot, what are you doing?* And I secretly call myself every horrible name in the book. I yell, I am furious, I feel so incompetent, and I can't find the energy to complete the job. And so I don't. I stop. I walk away and let someone else do it. But somehow, even though it took me almost two hours, I never did that to myself. I just completed it. And that is what made me feel so proud. I had made a lot of mistakes, but somehow I learned through it. They didn't stop me. I didn't let shame win. I let the failures come, and I gave myself grace. Eighty-nine minutes of grace. Hopefully I won't need as many minutes next time.

16

LEARNING

None of us ever went to school and learned the chemistry
of it from books. We learned the trick by doing it,
standing with our faces in the scorching heat while
our hands puddle the metal in its glaring bath.

James Davis, *Iron Worker*

Today young men seek salvation through glib answers and heady
beliefs in what Jesus did for them instead of walking the mystery
themselves, too. True religion is not about winning eternal life later
by passing some giant SAT now. It is about touching upon life now,
in this moment, and knowing something momentous yourself.

Richard Rohr, *Adam's Return*

These men knew paint. Carlos and John had spent hours and years
working with it. Brushing it. Sanding and spraying it on walls and

fences with the most intricate detail. They had cleaned it off spray guns and China-bristle brushes. Scrubbed it off their faces and skin each night. While interacting with these painters as they handled oil stain or latex primer, it hit me that I didn't know that much about paint—and that my understanding of paint was in some deep way a metaphor of my life.

All of my learning had been done at school. As a little boy I bonded with my school desk, my eyes fixed to a chalkboard and the information written on it (mostly by female teachers). It started with colors and animals in elementary school and transitioned to chemistry formulas, math problems, and the history of the Civil War in high school, and finance and marketing in college. I had spent nearly twenty years learning in this environment and thousands of hours doing homework outside of class.

My entire existence of learning was sitting in a chair.

It was a simple learning formula, I guess. I would walk in. Sit down. The teacher would stand up, and I would take notes. I would memorize facts and try to keep all of that knowledge in my head for the test. It was really the same scenario when it came to spiritual teaching. I had grown up listening to someone behind a pulpit as I sat in the pew. They spoke, and I took notes and learned about God, much like I would a formula for chemistry. In college many of the classrooms where I heard lectures were at night converted into locations for ministers, who taught their students in much the same way.

I took it all in. And I did well. For the most part it was about mastery. I made good grades. I grew in my understanding of people, ideas, things, God, and His Word. I was feeling knowledgeable—looking pretty good.

I thought I *knew* how to paint like I thought I *knew* about a lot of things. That was before I started painting. When I showed up at the job site, there was no classroom instruction by John or Carlos. No teaching or gentle introductions like so many of my female teachers in school had given me. I was to get to work and jump in. When I screwed something up, they told me, stopped their work, and taught me how to do it right. It seemed it was happening every hour. I was failing at every turn. Screwing things up. Missing caulk lines and spots on the wall.

The same thing was happening on the trout streams. A cold mountain river had thousands of places for a fish to hide: near boulders and banks or in deep pockets of dark water. You had to know exactly where they would be. You had to know how to place the fly right next to the trout's mouth. It required a specific fly—from a thousand possibilities that were determined by season, time, temperature, hatches, the placement of the line, and the dropper weight. I didn't know any of this when I started. I just wanted to catch large, lovely trout and be Brad Pitt in *A River Runs Through It*. But since the trout were not all that interested in my dreams, I needed help.

It was the same in hunting. I couldn't understand how to load a gun without Charles, Steve, or Mark helping me out. Men had to constantly teach me: grab my rod, brush, or shotgun, point out my errors, and instruct me. And while I was really grateful for all their help and wanted it, it was a struggle to accept and need them. I wanted mastery—not constant correction. As one of my friends, Dan, shared, I always thought the goal was independence—getting it right so I could go off on my own and not need help. And I continually did not know what I was doing. As much as I tried, I could not learn it from a book or from the sheet of paper given to me at the fly shop. I needed help in the moment I was struggling and failing. I needed a man next to me.

I wondered what it really meant to know about something. To deeply know. While I knew a lot from my time in the classroom, my new work experiences were making me question how relevant my classroom knowledge really was. I knew stuff. A lot of stuff. I made A's and B's, which meant I was supposed to know things. But that knowledge wasn't helping me. My education hadn't provided me with many tangible experiences, nothing that really grounded me, gave me roots. In *Emile*, Jean-Jacques Rousseau says a student "will learn more by one hour of manual labor than he will retain from a whole day's verbal instructions."[18] In *The Way of the Wild at Heart*, John Eldredge says that learning is "one part instruction and nine parts experience."[19] My life had been void of experience. I had all knowledge and no experience. Maybe nine parts knowledge and one part experience—and that was being generous.

In his book *Boys Adrift,* Dr. Leonard Sax writes, "If you ask a boy to read about the life cycle of a tadpole metamorphosing into a frog, but that boy has never touched a frog, never had the experience of jumping around in a stream in his bare feet chasing after a tadpole, he may not see the point." He goes on to write, "Dr. Wilson says that medical school instructors are having more difficulty teaching medical students how the heart works as a pump, 'because these students have so little real-world experience.' They've never siphoned anything, never fixed a car, never worked on a fuel pump, may not even have hooked up a garden hose. For a whole generation of kids, direct experiences in the backyard, in the tool shed, in the fields and woods, has been replaced by indirect learning, through [computers]. These young people are smart, they grew up with computers, they were supposed to be superior—but now we know that something's missing."[20]

Something is missing? Yep. It made a lot of sense why I knew so little about the real world around me. I had yet to experience it. It made we wonder if God had led me to paint, dirt, and trout to learn a few things I had missed.

If you look out at what men are lacking today, it often comes down to experience. My friend David, who works in the construction business, sent me this e-mail:

> Last Wednesday night, the guys from Sigma Chi Bible study all decided to come help me and Jason hang sheetrock on the ceiling. They showed up and hadn't been there forty-five minutes when Alex, a freshman, came and found me. He held his hand out for me to shake and said, "David, I just want to thank you for having me over here tonight." To which I replied, "Alex, are you leaving already?" He said, "No, not at all; I just wanted to tell you how great this is. I've never done anything like this at all, and never would have dreamed that I could do this kind of stuff. This is awesome. Can I come back and help some more?"

A man in Nashville who owns a law firm was telling me about his dilemma. He has been hiring dozens of young lawyers fresh out of school. He explained that despite their education, they had a hard time relating and talking to ordinary people—a jury. They were almost too smart for their own good.

The verb "to know" is fascinating because most languages have two words for it. Sax explains it this way:

> Most European languages use two different words for these two kinds of knowledge. In French, to know in the sense of knowing a person is *connaître*; to know in the sense of knowing a subject in school is *savoir*. In Spanish, to know as in knowing a person is *conocer*; to know in the sense of book learning is *saber*. In German, knowledge about a person or a place that you've actually experienced is *kenntnis* from *kennen*, "to know by experience"; knowledge learned from books is *wissenschaft*, from *wissen*, "to know about something."

ENGLISH	GERMAN	SPANISH
I know Sarah.	Ich *kenne* Sarah.	*Conzco* a Sara.
I know chemistry.	Ich *weissum* Chimie.	*Se* quimica.[21]

In biblical Hebrew the verb *lada'at,* "to know," refers primarily to experiential learning.

And that was the core problem with my painting. I knew about paint, but I didn't really know it. Not like the men I worked with, who had spent years interacting with it and scrubbing and mixing it. These experiences of knowing, truly knowing, were lacking in my life—and so many of us as young men had missed them. We had knowledge of things through books and the Internet, but not through working, failing, and getting our hands dirty.

I was getting to know paint by screwing it up and getting it on me. I was becoming intimate with paint. When I screwed up caulking the underside of a window trim, I was corrected and remembered it because I hacked it up last time and wasn't planning on making the same mistake twice.

The world wasn't grading on confidence or experience. It was grading on knowledge. Everyone was looking for the answers. Teachers wanted answers to essay questions. What is the theme of Shakespeare's *Sonnet 18*? An ionic bond? The impetus behind World War II? Even the way to get into a college was through a multiple-choice test. I made grades based on how much information I knew.

My report card was really based on intellectual performance— not physical aptitude or how I processed the information. It was about answers. I just did what I was told. The information went from the blackboard to our notes, our heads, and back onto the test, where it was graded based on how much of it was correct. The cycle was questions, then answers, then grades.

The word *failure* was pounded into me as the worst possible thing to get or become. If you failed, it meant you flunked the class.

You were stupid. You had to take the class again and didn't advance. To fail at anything in school meant you were in trouble. And for obvious reasons, the word became a symbol for the last thing you ever wanted to get.

The Scriptures are filled with men who encountered God. David G. Brenner writes in his book, *Sacred Companions,* "To really know God we must know his love experientially."[22] I never understood this. I took in knowledge through sermons and the stories of men like you might a math formula. It was inside me. But these were facts that I could recite, not a deep understanding.

As I read the story of David and Goliath, I noticed David had a deep knowledge of God because of his experience with Him. A rooted and settled confidence in God. We often recall his slaying the great giant. But what I never really saw in the story was what provided him with the confidence to slay the giant. It was his past, his experiences with God coming through for him before.

Saul replied, "You are not able to go out against this Philistine and fight him; you are only a boy, and he has been a fighting man from his youth" (1 Sam. 17:33).

Listen to what David gives as his reason:

> Your servant has been keeping his father's sheep. When a lion or a bear came and carried off a sheep from the flock, I went after it, struck it and rescued the sheep from its mouth. When it turned on me, I seized it by its hair, struck it and killed it. Your

servant has killed both the lion and the bear; this uncircumcised Philistine will be like one of them, because he has defied the armies of the living God. The LORD who delivered me from the paw of the lion and the paw of the bear will deliver me from the hand of this Philistine. (1 Sam. 17:34–37)

David goes back to his previous experiences to explain the future outcome.

We had no lions or bears. We had head knowledge. There is a settled confidence in the boy—he knows he has what it takes. But it is not an arrogance—he knows that God has been with him. He will charge Goliath and take his best shot, trusting God will do the rest. That "knowing" is what we are after ... and it only comes through experience.[23]

The act of knowing God looked less like a biology exam and more like Carlos experiencing paint or Ron experiencing the waters of the Arkansas River. Knowledge is based on experience and years, both of which I lacked. To gain knowledge of God, I would have to trust Him in situations that seemed doubtful and fearful. Situations in which the outcome was not certain, situations in which everything wasn't safe. Situations similar to David's, where God really needed to come through. I needed to go where I could be tested, where confidence and experience was found.

17

FATHERLAND

Father hunger is hard to talk about because it is
one of the most vulnerable parts of a man, his
desperate need for an older, wiser, or stronger man
to guide him, believe in him, affirm him, concretely
teach him, challenge him, and correct him.

Richard Rohr, *Adam's Return*

I have mentioned occasionally meeting with my mentor, John. One of his gifts is the ability to ask really good questions. I would share, enjoy being engaged, and walk out feeling alive. I cherished our time together.

But occasionally I wouldn't hear from him for a few weeks. The feeling that I mattered to him would start wearing thin. I would begin to question his validity as a man and many of the things he told me because he seemed so busy with other things. Though I'm not necessarily proud of it, I would start to wonder, *Maybe he really doesn't care about me. Does he ever pray for me, think of me?*

I wasn't sure.

I would start to feel my need to talk with him, just be in his presence again. I didn't care that I was mad at him or that I was frustrated; I was desperate. And I hated feeling desperate.

I would get worried that he didn't want to meet with me anymore, so I would call or e-mail and ask him to meet again. Each time he would gladly agree. We would meet and that same scenario would play out: talk, counsel, good questions, sharing. And I would feel good again, remembering all the reasons why I respected him and all the things he had done in my life. I would leave a happy man. I would start reading more of his books, talking to friends about him.

But the happy would wear off a few days or weeks later. *Where was he?* I would think. *Did he forget me?* This cycle was perpetual. I loved him and hated him.

My friend Ryan confessed he had yet to meet a man he would even want in his life. He was serious. His father got lost in drinking and adultery, leaving Ryan and his mother when he was young. I asked him about possible mentors. He said there was always something he didn't respect in every man he had met, some little character flaw. The flaw was just enough to disqualify the man. Ryan's life was filled with dozens of men, but they had all been crossed off the list, not worthy of his time.

Robert Bly asks when a son "does not see his father's workplace, or what he produces, does he imagine his father to be a hero, a fighter for good, a saint, or a white knight?" Bly's thought is that demons—demons of suspicion—move into that empty place:

> The demons ... encourage suspicion of all older men. Such suspicion effects a breaking of the community of old and young men ... Mentorship becomes difficult to sustain; initiation is rejected ... The son, having used up much of his critical, cynical energy suspecting old men, may compensate by being naïve ... Between twenty and thirty percent of American boys now live in a house with no father present, and the demons there have full permission to rage.[24]

It was true for me as well. I could probably list forty men that I had checked off for various reasons in the last eight years of my life, flawed men whom I had once wanted to teach and lead me. Maybe a man did not return my calls or e-mails for a few weeks, which in my head meant he was way too busy for me. Maybe a man was too heavy theologically, too religious and disciplined; or maybe he was too soft, too meek-and-mild-Jesus. He could have been way too driven, egotistical, or maybe completely out of touch. To some degree I'm not sure it mattered. In my head I sized them up and ran them through a gauntlet of impossible trials, then spit them out. And yet I both wanted and needed them. I had this deep inner hunger for male mentorship that drove me mad.

I could rattle off all the reasons men had failed my generation: how they were never home, out chasing success, pursuing worldly things as their wives and children suffered. I could also include all the sociological reasons beginning with the industrial revolution on down. But the passion behind my voice had as much to do with me as any injustice to my generation.

I haven't shared this story with you yet, but I think I need to. When I was in college a man on campus sexually abused me. He was not a dark figure who fit some profile of a child molester. He was actually far from it. He was a community leader who worked with students, many of them young men. A sharp guy, respected by all. I figured I could trust him.

He was a man who gave me great insight into my life and what paths I might choose. Besides a mentor named Rick, he was one of the first men who ever sought me out and asked me good, challenging questions.

I would often visit his house and eat meals with him. We would talk about ministry-related things, and I always sought his approval, his respect. I was at his house one night, reading to him some of my writing and wanting to hear his thoughts on it—deeply in search of his approval, desperately looking for answers. I was inviting him to validate my struggle. He asked me to sit near him on the couch and I did. As I began reading, he began to rub my back. I stopped reading, but he began moving his hand up my leg. I wasn't sure of his intention—I was very confused, but I trusted him. He kept going. It was so very awkward because I was delighted to be in this man's presence, so grateful for his hospitality and interest in me. I wasn't seeing it as wrong or bad—just confusing.

He then started moving his hand near my crotch. Bewildered, I stopped his hand and moved it away. I continued reading, not thinking much of it in the context of sexual abuse; I just thought it was awkward. But it was very weird. I gave him the benefit of the doubt. He had cared for me in so many ways. How could that have been any different?

You would think I would have been so angry, upset, and hurt about it, but I wasn't. Instead, without knowing it at the time, I made a simple vow: I would never again let a man get that close. While I was not sure what happened, I just knew I must never let it happen again.

Two years later I found myself at a conference led by Dan Allender, who was teaching on the topic of sexual abuse. I went to the conference not because I was all that interested in the topic but because, once again, I was drawn to a strong male figure. Dan was a seminary president and the author of many books I enjoyed. I wanted to experience his teaching and was hoping to meet with him too. But in the middle of the three-day speaking event, I realized I had been sexually abused. I also realized I had been set up. The man on campus had chosen me. Through all those years, conversations, and meals, he had been planning the abuse, drawing me in. He knew full well my deep hunger for male affirmation, and he abused it.

While in Colorado, I was seeing a female counselor. She had heard all my frustrations about these love/hate experiences with my mentor, John. She asked me, "Okay, then … So what do you want?" It seemed such a simple question. Finally a chance to air my true desire, put it out there, get it off my chest. But I just sat there. *What did I want from him?* I had never really thought about it. I wanted to meet with him more—I knew that. But she would say, "Well, what do you want more of?" And I would say, "More of his interest in my life." And she would say, "Why?" And I would just sit there, unsure, confused, silent. I had no idea.

After a few weeks of this back and forth, mostly me just sitting in awkward silence, I finally said, "I want to go on adventures with him. I want to go mountain biking and fly-fishing and rock climbing. He has never asked me to do any of those." I thought, *There it is. Finally I put it out there. I was being as vulnerable as I could and stating what I wanted from him.* And then she would ask, "Why again?" I didn't know.

She seemed to be getting at something important. But I had no idea what it was.

It was our last session when my counselor asked me again, "What do you want, Xan?" I talked circles around the question. And while I think she wished I would say it, our time was running out, so she finally said it for me: "Xan, you want this man to be your father."

I sat there for a while, thought about it. I did. While I never said it, never thought of it that way, it might be what I wanted, this man as my father. Okay, yes. I did. That was at the core of this deep longing inside me.

I let it settle for a few days and talked to Jayne about it. My counselor's words had struck a deep place in me. I decided to call John and asked him to meet. He agreed. I started talking to him, and after our time was almost over, I realized I had yet to say anything about what I really wanted from him. As I prepared to, I started feeling shaky. I stumbled a bit. I was fumbling with my words, so afraid and confused. He kept looking at me and saying, "I am not sure what you are asking, Xan." I think he was helping me along. And then finally I said, "I want to go mountain biking with you and maybe on some of your adventures." He sat there, pondering, then said, "Thanks for telling me. I'll pray about it." We parted ways after lunch.

I couldn't do it, couldn't voice my real desire. I was so mad. It was almost too much, too vulnerable. *What would he do with my real desire? What would he say?*

I told my counselor what happened, and she told me to go back again. So I called him up a few days later, feeling a bit like a fool, and asked if we could meet again. He agreed. And finally, in probably the most vulnerable and fearful moment of my life, I looked at him in the middle of some sushi restaurant and said, "I want you to be my father." I tensed up. Waited. He looked at me with a huge, warm smile. He was beaming with a look of understanding, like he knew this day was coming—as if he had a full awareness of the deep hunger inside of me. He said, "What a good desire, Xan."

He just kept smiling. I kinda felt like I was watching it all from a few tables away—watching him, observing myself not knowing what to do. I had told him. And he had just said my heart's desire was good. He never answered it. Never said he would meet that need. He just enjoyed that moment.

For the first time in my life, I had spoken my need without shame, and he had validated it. He told me it was good. It was one of the greatest days of my life. And while I had no idea what would happen next, I had named what I longed for: fathering.

18

BLOOD

Hunting is one of the few activities that allows an
individual to participate directly in the life and death
cycles on which all natural systems depend.

Ann Causey, philosopher

For the life of a creature is in the blood, and I have given it
to you to make atonement for yourselves on the altar.

Leviticus 17:11

My friend P.J. had invited me to accompany him on an elk rifle
hunt to an area of land known as Area 5-11, just outside of Divide,
Colorado. He had drawn a rifle tag for elk hunting and wanted me
to join him. I happily agreed.

We spent the evening traveling to an area called Hackett Gulch.
We were a few miles into the Colorado backcountry when P.J.

spotted an elk from a lookout atop a high ridge. I waited as he ran about 250 yards out of my sight to a clearing that gave him a visible shot across the valley. I heard the crackling thunder, then the rippling echo. Then another shot. P.J. descended into the ravine to look for the elk, and I ran to meet him. As the sun began to set he screamed from across the valley—the elk was down. I climbed down the deep ravine of jagged rocks, rushing to the other side to find him kneeling next to his bull elk.

There he was. I knelt down into the dirt and snow, exhausted from the steep climb and staring at the brown eyes of the elk lying lifeless before us. He was massive, a giant beast of the hills. I touched his limp carcass and ran my hands across his thick, warm fur like you might pet a dog. The blood from his fatal wound was splattered all around, coloring the white snow red like a cherry slushy.

As a kid I always did my best to avoid blood and pain and death. I never had any unusual blood lusts or attachments to death. Never had the addictive pull to kill soldiers in video games and watch blood spew, or to rent horror movies. And I wasn't one of those risk-taking kids who got cuts and stitches every few days like some daredevil Mountain Dew junkie. I grew up in the suburbs where things were pretty tame and controlled. As a boy, blood meant one thing: death.

As we moved around the elk, examining it, I had never felt so many mixed emotions—both remorse and excitement. It was a moment of joy and celebration for P.J., but I also realized a life had been taken. I had assisted. A soberness slammed into me, an ambivalence of joy, death, and pain. I related to C. L. Rawlings, who said, "I could see myself in those animals. What had been a game to me was suddenly not one. That's the worst part of hunting—to pull the trigger knowing what will result: pain, shock, blood, death."[25] Moments ago this beautiful animal was eating grass. Now its body lay twisted and contorted in the snow, outlined in blood. Dead.

Darkness was setting in, so P.J. wanted us to get to work. With only the two of us, it was all hands on deck to open the elk's body to keep the meat from spoiling. I listened and followed his instructions. We spread the rear legs wide and tied them to a tree with some rope— that gave us access to his belly. P.J. began cutting into his hide near the stomach. He made one long incision all the way up from his belly to his neck. It was like unzipping a fur coat. He cut some bone, then pop! The rib cage expanded, fanning out like a newly opened roll of refrigerated cinnamon rolls. As his hands plunged deep inside, steam and blood poured out. Fluids dripped from the body, and I heard some unusual noises. I would have been fine just observing. But he needed my help, and within a minute my hands were deep in the elk's body, feeling around for the esophagus and yanking on the gut bag with him to break it free from the body. The bag fell out like a massive water balloon with organs trapped inside, dropping into the snow next to us.

It was too dark to continue. And we needed more help to hike out the hundreds of pounds of meat anyway, so we took off to get some rest; we would come back in the morning with a few more friends. As we hiked, I had time to think. Such an unusual experience. I just had my hands two feet inside the body of a dead animal.

I hadn't known if I could actually do it. I figured I would pass out or turn into gelatin. But I didn't. The blood on my hands was turning dark brown, drying as I walked. I was proud to be wearing it. It was almost like a baptism.

We woke up early the next day and took to finishing the elk. Our buddies, Cory and Morgan, joined us as we hiked into the valley. We had a collection of saws, Buck knives, gut hooks—it looked like a portable butcher shop. We started peeling the hide and outer layer of fat away from the body. It was like pulling up a shag carpet from an old house. The muscles, tendons, ligaments, and joints and the fleshy red color of meat became exposed.

We began quartering the elk and cutting it into sections. We started sawing into leg bone, cutting off the feet, removing the ball joints to make the meat into hindquarters, separating it while ripping muscles and tendons, then placing them in large sixty-to-eighty-pound cotton bags in our packs. It was a pretty graphic scene. It wasn't like laying a steak on a grill or slapping together hamburger meat into round patties. There was sawing, cracking, ripping, and cutting to free the meat from tendons and bone.

While much could be talked about here, the irony of all this bloody mess is that the Bible is covered in it. There is more tragedy and death in Scripture than you might find in a horror movie. You'd be hard pressed to find a page where something or someone isn't dying, or blood isn't being shed on the account of the Israelites in the Old

Testament—or even more specifically, where animal sacrifice isn't taking place. It's not one of those things we like to highlight, but it is there. God almost seems obsessed with it. Blood and death, and the sacrificing of animals, might be argued as some of the most major themes of the Bible, especially the Old Testament. Alfred Edersheim, a Jewish scholar, writes, "Every unprejudiced reader of the Bible must feel that sacrifices constitute the centre of the Old Testament."[26]

The center? That's a big statement. This is no G-rated Disney special featuring Hannah Montana or the cast of *High School Musical*. It seems more like a horror flick. A love story, yes, but one with tremendous blood. Here is where the words *blood* and *death* rank with a few other big words of the Bible:

> *Love: 700 times*
> *Life: 589 times*
> *Death: 452 times*
> *Blood: 389 times*
> *Hope: 174 times*
> *Birth: 153 times*
> *Money: 114 times*
> *Sex: 56 times*

I can remember assisting with communion in our Anglican church, administering the cup. I would reverently say, "This is the blood of Jesus, shed for you." A whole line of people would pass the cup and repeat after me. But I tell you, I did not really connect to the blood of our great High Priest until being in that moment with the elk.

Eugene Peterson shares about his experiences growing up:

> My father was a butcher and owned his own meat
> market. I always thought of my father as a priest.
> He wore a white butcher's apron as he presided over
> the work of slaughtering heifers and pigs, dressing
> them out, cutting them up ... My father was a
> priest in our butcher shop, and I was with him,
> doing priestly work ... I grew up experiencing the
> sight and sound of animals killed and offered up,
> the smell of fresh blood and the buzz of flies. A
> bull on the altar of Shiloh couldn't have looked or
> smelled much different than a shorthorn heifer on
> the butcher block in our shop on Main Street ... It
> never occurred to me that the world of worship was
> tidy or sedate.[27]

While I was cutting up the elk with P.J., Morgan, and Cory,
there was something directly spiritual about it. It provided me with
a deep appreciation and understanding of the deep mystery of the
gospel, of life, pain, sacrifice, and blood all mixed together.

All this from getting blood on my hands.

19

MISTAKES

Would you like me to give you a formula for success?
It's quite simple, really. Double your rate of failure.

Thomas J. Watson, founder of IBM

I had never known a fighter pilot beyond Maverick of *Top Gun*—
not until my buddy Jonathan joined the air force. Flying jets had
been his lifelong dream. Jayne and I moved out to Colorado at
the same time he entered the service. He and I would occasionally
talk, and he would tell me about his travels and training adventures all over the country. One week he would be in Oregon at an
air force base; a few weeks later he'd be in New Mexico for g-force
training; yet another weekend he'd be in the desert for survival
training—not to mention all the weekends he spent flying jets all
over the country, learning new exercises and maneuvers from his
flight instructors.

Jonathan flies an F-15C, which is considered the best air-to-air fighter in the world. During the Persian Gulf War, the Iraqi Air Force wouldn't fight them; instead it buried its fighters in the sand. These aircraft win many fights by sheer intimidation. No one wants to go against them. Why? Because inside them are the world's best-trained pilots.

It was fascinating to hear him explain how they trained. Theirs was a culture based on the pursuit of perfection, impossible as it is to obtain. He once shared a story about a gathering of old veterans. Someone asked if they had ever flown a perfect flight. Their answer: no. They were constantly making mistakes while flying.

Most of the training comes by flying your F-15C jet (actually or in simulation) against more experienced flight instructors until you screw up or make a wrong move. When he screwed up, he would head back to base, then spend many hours going over his mistake in a debriefing time with his instructors. This would happen every day—over and over again. "We fail, we listen to our instructors, and we fail, and the instructors are right there to walk us through our mistakes," he said.

It was a culture in which people admitted their mistakes. Mistakes were not the end of the world—in fact, they were teachers. Instructors would lecture about their failures and mistakes so that their students would know better.

Jonathan explained, "The focus was not on what you did right— that was expected. It was talking through our mistakes."

I had always avoided mistakes, especially failure. Failing translated to being a failure; *making* a mistake to *I am* a mistake. I always found ways to avoid failure. My life centered on doing the things I was good at. Sticking with my gifts and talents and abilities.

I was asking a lot of guys my age, "What did you think about failure?" They also admitted they hated it, avoided it at all costs, and spent their lives focusing on their strengths.

I had never been in a learning environment in which the prerequisite to growth was screwing up—until now.

It was interesting to process what my buddy and his sixteen-million-dollar jet were saying by way of a twenty-dollar paintbrush and my painting crew. I could understand what Jonathan was saying. It was all on-the-job training. I was learning by getting in there and doing it—screwing it up and making mistakes that made the boss angry; or Carlos or John having to come over and school me on how to hold the brush at an angle to pull a straight line. I was learning everything by screwing it up, not doing it right.

It was everywhere I turned. It was an entire new way of learning—by doing. And screwing it up. And then doing it over and over again till I finally got it right.

It seemed ironic that while I was taught about Jesus in Sunday school rooms and auditorium seats, Jesus usually didn't use such methods to teach His disciples. Instead of taking them to classrooms, He took them *out,* letting them try on and sample the things of the kingdom. They would screw it up, then He would end up correcting, rebuking, and teaching them about what just had happened. It was really unbelievable to me how the Scriptures are filled with the disciples getting things wrong—almost constantly. It was almost embarrassing how horrible they were at understanding Jesus. I did a study and it seemed about 80 percent of what left their mouths, or their actions, was not right.

Here is a CliffsNotes summary of the Jesus-disciples interaction in the gospel of Matthew:

Disciples follow Jesus. But then they get afraid of the storm in a boat. Disciples wake up Jesus, and Jesus is not that happy about it. "You of little faith, why are you so afraid?" (Matt. 8:26). Jesus teaches in a few places, then sends his twelve disciples out to do the work He has been doing (Matt. 10). Jesus tells disciples not to send the people away hungry (the crowd of 5,000), but says, "You give them something to eat," as if trying to get them involved in the miracle of multiplying food, which seems foreign to them (Matt. 14:16). Peter walks on water with Jesus, but then begins to doubt, starting to be afraid on the water. Jesus says, "You of little faith," and, "Why did you doubt?" (Matt. 14:31). Jesus shares a parable, but Peter doesn't understand the parable, so he asks Jesus about it. Jesus says, "Are you still so dull?" (Matt. 15:16). Ouch. The disciples are worried about having enough bread to feed another crowd of four thousand. Maybe they could do with four thousand what they did with five thousand. But they don't.

Even after that, they forget bread for themselves on a trip and start worrying about being hungry again, and finally Jesus really goes after them:

> You of little faith, why are you talking among yourselves about having no bread? Do you still not understand? Don't you remember the five loaves for the five thousand, and how many basketfuls you

gathered? Or the seven loaves for the four thousand,
and how many basketfuls you gathered? How is it
you don't understand that I was not talking to you
about bread? (Matt. 16:8–11)

Finally after all this Jesus asks them, "Who do people say the Son
of Man is?" (Matt. 16:13). Peter says, "You are the Christ. The son of
the living God" (Matt. 16:16). Finally someone gets it! But in the next
story Peter rebukes Jesus, telling Him to not get Himself killed, and
Jesus says to Peter, "Get behind me, Satan! You are a stumbling block
to me" (Matt 16:23). This continues. The disciples can't drive out
demons. Jesus says this indicates a lack of faith. One of the disciples
betrays Jesus. Peter denies Jesus three times. They have trouble staying
awake while Jesus prays. And when Jesus is taken to trial, they all flee
in fear.

Now, hearing those stories, is it not unbelievable that these are
the men who take the message of Christ to the nations and become
the apostles of the church? They sound like idiots who fail constantly.
They net a few victories here and there, but they require almost constant correction and rebuking. The disciples were constantly getting
it wrong and missing the point.

Here were these men, these simple men, who kept screwing up.
And yet—and maybe this is the greatest tribute to their character—
they kept following Jesus. And Jesus kept teaching them. It was almost
as if getting it wrong, screwing it up, and failing were prerequisites
to discovery and spiritual growth. Discipleship seemed to be about
walking with each other, falling or failing, and getting back up to try
it again.

I had always thought of discipleship as sitting at Starbucks with my Bible open, studying the Word or memorizing Scripture. Most of the discipleship I was familiar with was accomplished by sitting, not doing. It wasn't about learning from my mistakes, but about getting things right. I had been following that model my whole life.

It made me wonder if the air force was doing a better job discipling its students than the church. Maybe failure was the key to increased faith.

Scott McWilliams, a Nashville father, told me a story about his sixteen-year-old son's summer job on a farm. It was a month-long gig that required him to cut thick brush and weeds. On his son's first day, Scott noticed he didn't have any water or gloves. Scott knew his son would need them. Scott's wife was worried, but he told her, "Let him learn this on his own."

Here's the CliffsNotes version: Son started working, immediately soaked in the humidity of the summer heat and blisters on his hands. He comes home and tells story to parents. The next day he grabs one bottle of water. Father takes him out to his pile of gloves and he lets son pick. Father notices son's choice is heavy, thick rubber gloves. Father lets son go to work. Son's mother worries. The next day, son comes to father for help. Father is happy to help. He waited for him to ask. He gives him a jug of water and some thin gloves.

As I listened to Scott's story, it all made sense. With no men around to guide us, no one to help us make mistakes and teach us, we do things on our own. We have had no experiences to fall back on. Most of my mistakes in college were made alone and brought incredible shame. There was no one there to interpret them, help me get back up, walk me through a few-hour flight debrief so I could learn. So, of course, I made sure never to repeat them. The guys I was around (myself included) weren't confessing our struggles and mistakes and learning from each other. We were doing our best to look good and fit in.

I heard in Scott's voice a father's desire for his son to learn. He was there to help and guide him so he could ultimately succeed. When his son failed, Scott was right there with him. He wanted him to learn, to ask. It sounded like true discipleship, like God's heart for His children.

Maybe this was God's heart for me. Maybe Jesus was willing to reinterpret my failures and help me see them differently.

20
MASTERPIECE

The men taught me to kill rabbits pretty well. But
that turned out to be the least of their hunting
knowledge and the least of what I would learn
from my years of hunting with the men.

Walt Harrington, *Everlasting Stream*

Dust swirled around, our truck's tires kicking it up behind us as we pushed deeper into the Colorado back country. You could hear the howl of wind blowing to the east, the October's freezing weather gathering ice on our windows as we snaked through old washboard back roads that spread through the wide-open ranch land of the West. No boundaries, no fences, no distracting signs and buildings to lure us off course. This was frontier: ponderosa pines and Douglas fir carpeting the surroundings out to the Sangre de Cristo Mountains rising in the distance.

My buddy Cory had invited me to his family's annual elk-hunting camp. It was a tradition older than me. I was eager but nervous. Cory's father, Earl, along with Richard, Woody, his son Dwayne, and many working-class and laboring men had, over the past quarter century, migrated to this remote location to hunt elk and mule deer.

Although I was going hunting, I was without a gun. It seemed odd, with the thousands of dollars worth of gear I had collected, but I was going to follow along and observe. I left my rifle at home. It was a decision I made for many reasons, one being that I was starting to see that I needed hunting as much for the process as for a mounted trophy elk for our living room. It felt like repentance for me. I wanted to learn from men who had been doing this for so many years, to be attentive to their stories and techniques, to understand more about what this experience really meant. I couldn't do all that alone at the range. Jere thought I was crazy for doing this. "You go hunting to hunt," he'd say. But I was beginning to think differently.

I had learned this in part from spending time with a fine furniture maker named Dan—one of Cory's friends who is in his fifties. He owns land an hour from my home, and there he works with wood—not production pieces, but unique, museum-quality furniture showpieces. Everything about his work is intentional. He designs each piece, deciding every detail before he makes a cut. He likes listening to Mozart or Bach while he shapes and cuts and sands.

I was over at his house one day for lunch when he asked me, "Have you ever heard of a masterpiece?"

I nodded yes.

"Well, do you know where that term came from?"

I did not.

He explained, while chewing on some fresh sausage on his front porch, that during the Renaissance, there was a large culture of craftsmanship; folks took pride in good, honest work. Items— clock or a shirt—were not manufactured on assembly lines, but created by the hands of individuals. In fact there were blacksmiths, furniture makers, silversmiths, saddlers, butchers, rug makers, wood carvers, shoe peddlers, tailors, and painters, all in small stores scattered across Europe. But one didn't just set up a shop and go into business on a whim. No, there was a process a man had to go through to establish himself in a trade. He had to be a master to have his own place. The masters had trained in their crafts for most of their lives. You would almost always find young apprentices working near a master, many times his own son. Apprentices would spend thousands of hours and many years with the master, watching, learning, and doing their part.

Their part often consisted of simple and menial tasks like sweeping sawdust off floors or organizing tools. Mundane work. An apprentice became the master's right-hand man. But the master was aware that his knowledge about his craft was limited; there were so many unique expressions, styles, and ways to make the crafts and items. So the master would send his apprentice off to be with other masters at other shops in nearby cities. They called these young men *journeymen*. It was only after thousands and thousands of hours spent with many different men in many different cities that a young man's work would be seen as credible. Eventually he would create his own masterpiece using the skills of all the others who had poured their knowledge into him.

I listened to Dan talk with this stirring in my heart. I had never experienced anything like that. What would it have been like to try and fail and learn under other men—so many men? Not just one man, but to be sent all over the country, learning from other men too? I was lucky to find one good man or mentor, let alone a whole group of them. I wasn't even dreaming that big. But there seemed to be something to this process, this learning at the feet of men, moving into your own unique, creative talents and gifts. It was something I knew I had missed.

Dan believes that most guys fresh out of school believe they are ready to become masters without going through the process. I laughed. That was me, though I did not tell him. He believes most of us young men have never had older men around to teach us. As Robert Bly explains, "The traditional way of raising sons, which lasted for thousands and thousands of years, amount to fathers and sons living in close—murderously close—proximity, while the father taught the son a trade: perhaps farming or carpentry or blacksmithing or tailoring." The goal was not just the transmission of a trade. It seemed that something happened when boys and fathers were together—like Bly says, "A substance almost like food passes from the older body to the younger."[28]

I had never interacted with men in this way. There was the occasional coach, but my jobs and experiences rarely included older men. In fact there were only six male teachers I had ever rubbed shoulders

with. Even then the interaction was through notes and lectures, trading remarks on paper.

In his book *Boys Adrift,* Sax writes about a native Alaskan recounting
his life of hunting:

> "When I was growing up," he told me, "I learned
> to hunt the sea lion with the older men of the tribe.
> I learned about patience. I learned about using my
> senses. All my senses. I would go out on the ice with
> the older men and we would sit for hours, waiting
> for the sea lion. Hours … We were silent. We were
> aware. I could sense the sea lion approaching when it
> was still five miles distant. I can't tell you how I did
> that, but there is no doubt that I knew, with absolute
> certainty, when the sea lion was approaching … Our
> traditional life depended on the sea lion.
>
> "… You must kill the sea lion at precisely the right
> moment. Its lungs must be filled with air. Otherwise
> the animal will sink to the bottom when you shoot
> it and you will not be able to retrieve it. You must
> be patient. You can't shoot it as soon as you see it.
> You must wait for it to take that deep breath …
> Then the leader will give the signal."

"He tells you when to shoot?" I asked.

"He doesn't say anything. You watch him out of the corner of your eye. He fires first—then all of us fire within a tenth of a second of his shot. All the shots hit the animal in the head. That's how it is supposed to be. And that's how it was, every time. The animal dies instantly, floats on the water, and we retrieve it."

"So what's different about the young men you saw?" Larry had said something during the meeting about how the young men in his tribe now insist on going out on their own. They don't want any guidance from the older men, and the lack of guidance shows in the way they hunt the sea lion … Those young men were talking. Laughing. Joking. Punching each other … They weren't watching the sea. They weren't paying attention to the wind. They were never quiet. A sea lion appeared and they didn't even notice. Then one of them saw it and yelled. They all grabbed their guns and started shooting wildly. They didn't kill it. They wounded it. It swam away …

Fifty years ago, Larry explained, young men and old spent whole days and nights together in traditional underground structures they called "men's houses." In these small, confined spaces … the art of hunting was passed from one generation to the next."[29]

These stories made an impression on me. I wanted what Dan the crafts-man talked about: the process. The journeyman phase. It is why I wanted to be out in the middle of the woods with these men. And on the rivers. I wanted to learn to hunt the sea lion, to wait and watch the weather, and at the right moment, to fire. I needed older men to help me.

I think that is what also fascinated me about Ron, and his fly shack, and fishing with him. He had been fishing for over fifty years, ever since he was four years old. His father had taken him on these same rivers to fish. He can still recall the memories of driving by streams, seeing his father out on the waters. It was a collected skill that Ron and his fishing buddies Vern and Timm brought with them. It was the same with these elk hunters. These men had been hunting this land longer than I'd been alive. They were masters at their talents. And you could feel their wisdom by just stepping in their camp, or on the river with them. I just wanted to be near them, ask them questions, and watch them.

You could tell by watching Earl, Woody, and Richard at the hunting camp that they had been doing this for years. Their rug-ged, worn-out, rusted gear was proof. It was not clean and shiny like my gear. The canvas tent purchased at Cabela's years ago, once a white canvas, had been permanently stained brown and a dusty gray from dirt, the weather, fires, and years of heavy use. The grill with a custom pulley system, located over the fire pit, had been designed by Richard, who used some old steel pipes. The metal wire and grate of the grill was slowly rusting from many years of use. The aluminum cooler, trailers, and stoves were also Richard's creations.

I think that is why I loved being in the woods with them. Every time I walked into the worn tent that was the mess hall, I found these old relics, found myself entering into something much larger, much older than myself. There was something comforting in that; it didn't start with me and wasn't going to end with me either. These were traditions and rituals and stories that were still being passed down. I had joined in for only a moment's time, but it felt like I was experiencing God's hand on me like an aged, wise father—maybe like a great-grandfather—with strong, inviting, calloused hands, moving me a bit closer to the fire and the men. And some of what I had missed.

21

INVITATION

I go among trees and sit still.

Wendell Berry, *A Timbered Choir*

Back in Nashville, Jeremy had caught wind that I was hunting. We were high school buddies and college roommates—good friends, but very different. I chewed spearmint gum. He chewed Skoal—long-cut, straight tobacco. I listened to Pearl Jam and Dave Matthews; he listened to Waylon Jennings, Merle Haggard, David Allan Coe, and Hank Williams Jr. I went golfing in my Polo shirts, and Jeremy went hunting in full camo. In high school I had always made fun of Jeremy for hunting, calling it a "redneck sport." He would wake up early and sit in his deer stand with his dad before class, often showing up an hour or two late. In college he returned the favor by making fun of me when I dressed up in my signature pink tie, pretty boy hair, and leather suspenders to announce something on behalf of our fraternity at the sorority hall. He found it ironic and deeply satisfying that I had joined his side and taken up arms.

He was so excited that he invited me to go deer hunting with him on his family land in Franklin, Tennessee, with two of my old fraternity brothers, Graham and Michael. The plan was to stay in the old, broken-down, "you wouldn't want to put your pet gerbil in there" trailer.

This was my first time actually hunting. In some ways I was really eager to prove myself. No pink ties this time. No getting made fun of for being the pretty boy. I took my accumulated hunting gear and accessories—and experiences with P.J., Earl, Woody, and Dwayne—and packed them in this large duffel bag purchased specifically for the trip. Of course I had to include my shiny new rifle that I put into a shiny new plastic hard case. I walked into the Denver airport the morning of my trip, imagining Charlton Heston and Clint Eastwood coming up and giving me a strong "welcome, son" nod.

Jeremy greeted me at the Nashville airport. But there was a problem: They couldn't find my bags. It had been a routine flight with no gate changes—a straight flight. I had arrived at the check-in with plenty of time to spare. There seemed to be no explanation. The airline didn't know either. They told me they would send my bags to me when they arrived. *To a backwoods trailer?* I thought. *In the middle of nowhere? Down a bumpy dirt road?* This could not be happening. There was no way I was going to be hunting by opening morning. My bag of camo, my rifle, all my accumulated masculinity and security was missing, maybe even lost forever. I felt disoriented. Frustrated. Powerless.

What would I do?

Jeremy gave me a "no worries" look as we jumped in his red Dodge truck and took off to his trailer in the backwoods. I had nothing but the shirt on my back.

We settled in, met up with Graham and Michael, and had a good night, swapping stories from our glory days in college. I kept waiting, looking out the window for the taxi to come down the dirt road with my bags. It got later and later, and we finally called it a night. Jeremy assured me I was fine. They would figure out something in the morning.

The bags had still not arrived by the time we woke up. *What is this about, God?* I thought. *Why this?* Jeremy, Graham, and Michael started pulling stuff out of their bags and handing it to me: long underwear, a camo shirt, a hat, and some blaze orange. Jeremy grabbed his gun, put it in my hands, and started walking me to my spot: the best piece of land on the farm, guaranteed to get a deer. He climbed up the tree stand right behind me, pointed out the locations at which to look, walked me through it all, and then went back down to the trailer to wait.

Then I was alone: nothing but cold and darkness. I couldn't see anything. Nothing was moving. When you sit in a deer stand, you do just that. You sit. You sit on a cold and stiff metal seat that supports you. There is nowhere to move, and you have to be still so as not to spook the deer. You are given a few square inches of unforgiving uncomfortability. You are dozens of feet off the ground, hanging off the edge of what seems like a diving board in the woods, praying you don't fall asleep and plunge to your death.

Jeremy had told me to watch the land around me, but I couldn't see it yet. That would change soon. The deer would appear as the rising sun peeked its head over the landscape. Deer are generally night feeders, so it is the dawn and dusk hours, as the light awakens and fades, that bring hunters the best chance to nab one.

Within minutes sounds began to emerge from the blackness. The birds began to sing. A squirrel seemed to be collecting nuts in the leaves below, crinkling them as he moved through. I could imagine valleys and hills around me.

Just then the darkness gave way to light. It was rather poetic. *Maybe God had thwarted my bags from arriving?* I thought.

I was wearing another man's jacket and holding a rifle that was not mine. I had nothing. It was as if God said, "Xan, I lost your bags. I know you thought you could buy this experience, but you can't. This is a gift from My hand, an invitation."

I was supposed to be spotting the deer through Jeremy's borrowed binoculars, but I was too stunned by what was happening to me. I was being invited into something, not of my own or by my might. All that gear and the accumulation of tools in my garage was just my way of trying to buy the experience.

Here I was with nothing, yet feeling as if the whole world was before me. I had what I needed. God had provided it. My friends had helped me. I didn't need a thing; as Jeremy would say, "No worries." I was supposed to be looking for a big buck, but all I could do was smile, journal, and enjoy what was awakening around and inside of me. Pathetic maybe. But I didn't even want to shoot a deer anymore. I was there to learn a simple lesson: This was much bigger than killing something.

Later that day a taxi carried my bags down the dirt road to the house. I opened my bag while Graham, who had been hunting for years, looked through my collection of camo and gear. In his Southern drawl he said, "Shoeewt, Hood. You've got more gear than I do." I laughed and realized how foolish I was. We spent the evening eating day-old, greasy, mushy onions and potatoes and some of Jeremy's venison, listening to Hank Williams and Credence Clearwater Revival. I was full and taken care of in this old, musty backwoods trailer. And the last thing I was thinking of was killing a deer.

22

CURSE

Tom appeared on the sidewalk with a bucket of
whitewash and a long-handled brush. He surveyed
the fence and all gladness left him, a deep
melancholy settled down upon his spirit. Thirty
yards of board fence nine feet high. Life to him
seemed hollow, and existence but a burden.

Mark Twain, *The Adventures of Tom Sawyer*

The very ground is cursed because of you.

Genesis 3:17 MSG

I always believed that laboring at a working-class job hour after
hour and week after week would eventually cause a man to keel
over and die from exhaustion and boredom. My own work was
often tedious and lonely, not to mention the futility of activities

like watching the forty-mile-per-hour winds blow my plastic covering off for a wasted half a day's work, or spilling paint off the third story roof and seeing it splatter on the concrete below. Even worse: watching paint dry.

I found myself complaining a lot. I was becoming a jerk. I was cursing at my coworkers under my breath and at my boss, Mike, for working us so hard with no affirmation. Mike would tell us to "go faster," then later critique us for the sloppy work that happened because of a faster speed. Finally I asked, "What do you want: more quality or faster production?" He just looked at me with a devilish grin: "You will figure it out." I fumed. It was a no-win scenario. I hated this job.

My friend Dan Rieple, the fine furniture maker, believes you beat the selfishness out of people through hard work. He believes our generation has not learned this lesson, mainly because we have not worked hard, not worked with our hands, and not felt pain. It was obvious to all that I had never had that teacher, never been taught that in a class.

I was cursing the curse. If we look back in Genesis to the fall of Adam and Eve, we see they're banished from Paradise. Their sin separated them from God, and God removed them from His presence. But it doesn't end there. We find the Lord like some school principal, giving each party involved a curse, a consequence for their actions—even Satan.

The CliffNotes version of Satan's curse: "You will crawl on your belly." Eve's curse: "You will have pain in childbirth." And then

Adam's curse: "Cursed is the ground because of you; through painful toil you will eat of it all the days of your life. It will produce thorns and thistles for you, and you will eat the plants of the field. By the sweat of your brow you will eat your food until you return to the ground, since from it you were taken; for dust you are and to dust you will return" (Gen. 3).

For a loving God to do this seems pretty harsh. Those words— "Painful toil … thorns and thistles … sweat of your brow you will eat … dust you are and to dust you will return"—are strong. While there is plenty to unpack and explore in the verse, our first reaction has to be, *This is some heavy stuff.* As Pastor Tim Keller says, "Thorns will come up instead of fruit."

But it didn't start this way. Work at creation was designed to be rewarding, enjoyable, and fruitful. It was a pleasure and joy to work. But the curse changed all that.

It was as if He was creating the perfect storm for man's anger: work.

I didn't want to be such a downer, but I was. My painting job was hard. I experienced pain and frustration more than instant gratification or pleasure. There was no evidence that the work was important to God, or me, and it sure wasn't the way to get rich. All I could see was paint on a brush and wasted days. Hours passed by for nothing. It felt like a downward spiral. When I worked hard, I made nothing extra in return.

The work kept stirring up emotions and frustrations that I could not seem to shake, that I did not like, and that I wished would go away. Pessimism stuck with me as I rolled walls and painted trim and hated it all.

I related the experience to the words of Robert Bly in *Iron John*: "The way down and out usually separates the young man from his companion flyers and from their support, and it makes him aware of a depression that may have been living unnoticed in him for years. A mean life of ordinariness, heaviness, silences, cracks in the road, weightiness, and soberness begins."[30] I had never before felt such futility and boredom. I was now forced to feel the pain that before had always been dampened with new things, activities, and stuff. These cracks and hard places in me that I had never felt were now being exposed because, of all things, a job. It seemed to have very little to do with the actual work I was doing and more to do with me and something on the inside that I could not avoid.

With some help from my counselor and my wife, I was starting to admit that I was an angry young man. Richard Rohr believes that there is something behind anger: pain. And that you can't get rid of the pain until you learn what it has to teach you. Pain, like most of my emotions, was something that, as a man, I was supposed to rise above. There seemed nothing spiritual in feeling pain; it only made things worse. It was the opposite of hope and love. But Rohr says, "If you don't transform pain, you will transmit it." And that was it for me. I realized I was transmitting my pain through bad moods and tempers. It was probably why I had thrown lamps and coffee tables around the house in fights with my wife and why I had an addiction with pornography. There was something inside me that was hurting, but I never knew to identify it or what to do with it.

Men weren't supposed to cry, hurt, or feel pain, right?

I began wondering why I had rarely heard about the curse and its dreadful proportions. I could barely find books talking about regular work. There were books on finding your calling, your destiny, or pursuing your dreams, making millions, but nothing about just normal work—about a simple job like painting and how it related to God.

The more I searched, the more I wondered if history was one long avoidance of the curse. We seem to spend our lives trying to get away from the harsh realities of work and what it causes in us. Our system of life—economy, capitalism, and the soul's journey—seems to have been set up, in part, to find ways to get around it. Even the promise of retirement is that you are done with work.

I did some research, went through some books, and began to see that our views of work began to take shape a long time ago. Arguably, the greatest influence on American culture and society was Greco-Roman culture. The Greeks and Romans impacted arts, architecture, and intellectual thought. Even the New Testament was written in Greek. Their ideas spread through much of the Western world into the Renaissance and eventually to America. And what did they think of all this work back then—those fathers of our ideas? The great Greek philosophers Aristotle and Plato thought the most valuable pursuits were those of the mind. If you could be freed from all the rest of life's worries—all that painful, frustrating labor—you could pursue intellectual endeavors, the highest of opportunities. Pastor Tim Keller, in one of his sermons on work, says, "In the Greco-Roman world, manual labor was seen as demeaning. Work that didn't use your hands was more noble, and digging in ditches was dehumanizing." They saw the mind as the great pursuit, not the body or its function with work. Can you blame them? Smart people finding a way to avoid all that crap—of course!

So all the smart people were doing all this thinking while the second-class citizens, who could not afford to be educated, seemed to have no real voice, mainly because they were off working the fields, earning a living.

By this way of thinking, contemplation became exalted. It was all about getting yourself out of work, letting others do simple, mundane, repetitive tasks so you could move to a much higher calling. I realize this is sounding preachy, but stay with me a minute; there really is some good stuff here. The other problem is that for hundreds of years, the church was where young boys were taken to become educated in writing and study. While this was good on some levels; it was not so good on others. It took them out of normal work and put them in desks and in pulpits. All the other kids were out in the fields.

You can only imagine that with little experience in the material world combined with the curse, their preaching was consistently void of any experience of the harsh manual labor of the common people. Look at all the ornate, colorful, decadent robes of high-church priests and pastors. Their pristine garments seem to come from the thousands of years of avoiding not sin, but common physical work. You can see it in some of the thinking of the time. Saint Thomas Aquinas believed work could distract men from God: "The contemplation of divine truth … is the goal of the human life."[31] And Augustine: "The contemplation of God is promised as the goal of all our actions and the eternal perfection of happiness."[32] Even the kings of the time hired out the monks to do all the spiritual work (praying and fasting): "Since the lion's share of the choir monk's time was now taken up with reading, recitations, and prayers, there was little time left over for manual labor."[33] By the late Middle Ages, the monks were no longer working, "living on alms rather than earning one's living by the work of one's hands ... Manual work ceased to be the object of attention: ecclesiastical tasks came to be considered the only really sanctifying ones. This in effect closed the way to recognition of the sanctifying value of everyday work."[34]

A massive separation between work and God was formed.

So who does all the labor that is pointless and meaningless and of no religious value? The answer that ancient Greek society gave to this question can be summarized in a word: *slaves*. As America was being newly settled from Europeans, there weren't enough people to be laboring in fields, planting seeds, harvesting tobacco, sugarcane, and cotton. It seemed for many the answer was get someone else to do it.[35]

We could go on. While I am for progress, it seems that every invention and technological advancement in America seems to be connected to the promise of less work—letting the machines do the work for us. The industrial revolution was about building the skill into the machines.

Now I don't want to knock pastors or rich people; they work extremely hard in many different ways. Their work is not at all evil— not by any means. They labor just as the curse relegated them to, and we do need all types of classes and workers. But it seemed even Scripture shows the necessity of being connected to real physical work, even if just for a season.

The apostle Paul, the great author and voice of the gospel, made tents. David was a shepherd. Moses spent time with flocks of sheep. And maybe our greatest example, Jesus, spent the majority of His life in the great spiritual service of cutting and sanding wood as a carpenter. In fact, many people saw Him as simply "the carpenter's son" (Matt. 13:54–55).

And God, the great Creator Himself, is a worker too, as Pastor Tim Keller shares in one of his sermons: "At the beginning of Genesis you have God with his hands in the dirt. God just not in contact with physical, but becoming physical. This is an amazing statement of the dignity of all work; cleaning a house or making shoes is making order out of chaos. Even simple work, manual work, images the creator."[36]

I kept hearing about guys graduating college and wanting to go immediately into seminary or graduate school. While I could relate, and I can't judge their motives, I thought maybe, like me, they just needed a job, to spend a few years working with a hammer or a paintbrush, maybe making tents. It just might help their sermons one day.

Richard Rohr says there are two paths to God: the path of prayer and the path of suffering and hardship. God really wants us to find Him through prayer, but most of us, stubborn and hardheaded, only learn the hard way. It is as if the curse was God's way of bringing us into that pain, drawing us closer to Him. I could see that I was trying, at all costs, to avoid feeling and dealing with the curse. And I was also beginning to see that doing so was also avoiding God.

It all hit home for me one day on the job with Carlos. We were listening to a Spanish radio station, La Boom. The news came on, and while I could not understand Spanish, I could understand *Bush* and *immigration*. I asked Carlos what he thought about it all. He said to me, "I really don't understand Americans and how you treat us. You tell us to leave your country. But we are here working long, hard hours, and for a cheap price, doing the jobs none of you want to do." I stared at Carlos like one might stand before a great king with honor and respect. He was right. How could I argue that?

Maybe this was one of the reasons why I was here. There was something beautiful about this man, who was teaching me through his life and labor. Maybe this was as important a deed and task as any I completed in school. It was boring, hard, and long. And I didn't really like it. But it was as spiritual an act as prayer or preaching. He was inviting me into work—simple, basic, holy work.

23

CLOTHES

The soul of this man is in his clothes.

William Shakespeare

John's clothes were made of camel's hair, and he had a leather
belt around his waist. His food was locusts and wild honey.

Matthew 3:4

Although I can't confirm it, I think I might have been birthed wearing a Ralph Lauren Polo shirt. What I do know is that my parents
grabbed my tiny body and put me in outfits that had a little icon of
a man with a club sitting on a horse. I have the pictures to prove it.
Who or what the symbol was, I had no idea at the time. But I wore
them. And I kept wearing them on through college.

By the time I reached college, it was rare to see me without a
Polo symbol somewhere on my body. It was like my gang symbol.

My Polo collection consisted of everything from long-sleeve button-ups and cologne to beach towels and underwear. It was an important piece of my identity. Ralph and I were tight.

I wore other designer brands, but Polo was my bread and butter. Each knit shirt cost between fifty and sixty dollars retail, sometimes a little cheaper at another clothing store or on sale. But I needed the logo, whatever the price. And I wasn't really buying it anyway—my parents were. So I never thought too much about it.

When it came to painting, my job required me to wear white painter paints and a white shirt. No logo. No flashy symbols like Polo horses. Just white, plain white, like all the other painters who had gone before me. I had been told to go to Walmart and find a pair of white painter pants. I had never worn such a basic uniform in all my life. And I had never worn clothes from Walmart.

But the more I painted, the more I started to love my plain, white painter pants from Walmart. I was wearing those pants, sweating in them, getting deck stain and paint on them for a week without washing them. I observed the ritual of peeling them off each night and putting them back on in the morning; they were becoming worn.

Days and weeks of colors were appearing on the pants like an archaeological record of my work experience. And while they often smelled and stayed dirty, I actually loved putting them on. I was starting to become proud of my new work clothes—my Walmart work clothes.

I thought I was losing my mind.

◗

That pair of pants was really the first item of clothing that was not purchased for style or fashion, but function. When it comes to clothes, I tend to side with Thoreau:

> I say, beware of all enterprises that require new clothes, and not rather a new wearer of clothes. If there is not a new man, how can the new clothes be made to fit? If you have any enterprise before you, try it in your old clothes. All men want, not something to do with, but something to do, or rather something to be. Perhaps we should never procure a new suit, however ragged or dirty the old, until we have so conducted, so enterprised or sailed in some way, that we feel like new men in the old, and that to retain it would be like keeping new wine in old bottles. Our moulting season, like that of the fowls, must be a crisis.[37]

I was using them for their original design—not because of a look. I had never experienced that. My clothes were always purchased with a style in mind, to impress people, make my butt round, or hide my skinny legs. I know that may sound crazy, but it's true.

If you think about it, most clothes began with a function in mind. They had an original design. I bought carpenter jeans in college and enjoyed their thick canvas, but never knew that they were called carpenter pants because they were made for a carpenter. The loop on the pant leg—I never knew it was put there to hang a hammer on. I just thought that it was a cool name and that the loop was a style thing. And my cargo pants? No cargo placed in those pockets—simply another cool look to try and get the ladies to like me. Even all those jeans we Americans love, with the rugged, cotton-blue denim and metal-snap rivets: Those were originally made for men who worked on the decks of ships and underground in mines. Makes you kind of wonder about what those men would think of embellished jeans with glitter and fancy stitching.

One thing I've noticed is just how many men—blue-collar workers—don't really change styles. In fact you can't even say the word *style* in front of them without getting punched. Earl wore simple tube socks, and he had been wearing the same pair of jeans from Costco for the past ten years. Same look. When the jeans started ripping from frays and physical use, his wife would go and buy a new pair for fourteen dollars.

There is something right about that—a man not trying to chase down the latest fashion trend that will inevitably change every few months. A man who doesn't is stable, grounded, "of this Earth." So much of my life was spent trying to stay connected and look the part. But Earl was just Earl. He had a mustache, and I doubt that was ever in style. But I don't think he cared.

It was the same with Ron, my fishing partner. While Ron did own a Polo shirt, it was rugby style with those shoulder-pad-looking-things that were popular when I was ten, sometime back in the '80s.

I just don't think he really cares. Don't get me wrong: Ron does care, but not about style or fashion.

I surprised myself one day in Walmart when I found a shirt I liked in the men's department for eight dollars. It wasn't even on sale. Just eight dollars. It had a pattern that looked a lot like my Polos, a collared, button-up shirt. I put it on. I bought it and started wearing it. A shirt from Walmart to wear "out." To be honest, I bought a few more of them. For the same price as a Polo, I could buy five or six. It felt liberating.

I walked into a coffee shop one day and the hip young guy behind the counter asked about my two-pocket, long-sleeve shirt. "Hey, is that vintage Banana Republic?" he asked. I shook my head with a smirk. "Actually, no. Walmart. Eight dollars." He looked at me funny.

I was looking at my closet of designer shirts. Years of collected shirts. I can remember in college stocking up with my parents' money, knowing I would have them in my collection for the years ahead. I decided to put them in trash bags. I gave them to my wife and told her to take them to Goodwill. I couldn't look at them anymore. A few days later I asked if she got a donation receipt and she said, "Oops."

I can't help but notice that we all seem to crave something that has been worn, something authentic. No one wants a new pair of blue jeans. We want them to look worn and tattered. There's sandblasting, fading, and cutting. My friend David, a contractor, says that instead of wearing them into that look, we just want to buy them that way. It saves us time and effort. He thinks we don't want to have to go through the process or wait for the jeans to age. We want them quick, without the pain and work involved to get them there.

It all became personal a few months ago. I was at some outlet mall with my wife in her hometown in Pennsylvania. One of the stores specialized in Polo. I hadn't been in Polo in awhile. My beloved Polo. I felt like I should look around and check up on the place like you might an old girlfriend. I walked around, looking at the shirts and racks of clothes, all embroidered with the little horse. There was a display rack with some white pants. I approached, took them off the rack, and looked at them. They were white painter pants. White Polo painter pants. I couldn't believe it. I read the tag: "The rugged character of well-worn denim. Each piece a true individual, each with a story to tell."

I sat in my old, beloved Polo store that had bolstered my identity for so long, staring at this metal display rack and these pants, reading their promise to me: *"Rugged character. A true individual ... with a story to tell."* Wow. They were selling a promise. I smiled because I knew that promise could not be bought. It was something you had to walk through and earn.

24

SHAME

Shame is a silent killer ... Like a play, the curtain
parts and on center stage for all to see is a sight
that provokes condemnation and disgust.

Dan Allender, *Wounded Heart*

I got a call from Gil, my friend who lives in Denver and owns a bike
shop there. His store specializes in mountain and road bikes and was
in the process of expanding. He needed some extra hands to help finish the metal wall-board displays before the store's grand reopening.
He asked if I could come up with my friend Cory and install the wall
units. A two-day job. We gladly agreed.

The next morning Gil took us through our job. We were going
to take eight-by-four-foot sheets of MDF panel board, screw them
in, and handsaw each individual metal sleeve that slid into the long,
narrow slots of the MDF so the products could hang on. He took

us to the back of the store and into the bike repair shop to give us a workstation. The place was immaculate, like the garage I had always wanted: every type of tool hanging off pegboards, numbered, coded, organized, shiny, and neatly put into its place. There had to be ten or twelve workstations. Guys gathered around their workstations, busy repairing bikes, replacing spokes and front shocks, putting on new brakes. The shop was buzzing with activity and life and music.

Gil grabbed some of the tools we needed—a saw and a few metal files—and cleared off one of the workstations. We went to work, moving back and forth from the back to the front, putting up pieces, going back to cut metal pieces so we could put up the next. Cory and I were alternating. One would measure, saw, file; the other would head out from the repair shop into the retail store to put in a few metal slots, then head back to the repair shop to do it all over again. While I was no skilled craftsman, I was doing all right.

But as I went back into the shop near the end of the day, as Cory was out mounting one of the boards, I noticed the two metal files I had just been using were missing. I looked around the bench, but they were nowhere. I worked awhile, cutting the metal pieces but not finding the file to use. *Where did it go? Did I lose it? Did someone take it?*

A minute later one of the repair guys came around the corner on his way out the door. He looked over with a face of disgust and announced his frustration. Above the noise and buzz of the shop, he said, "That was a new file you were using. We replaced the old one because people were filing it just like you." Then he walked out the door—and disappeared. I stood there looking at the empty door, then burying myself in work, afraid to look around at all the other men, who had become quiet. The area was small enough that you could feel the silence and awkwardness around the shop. What had I done?

Cory came back into the shop as I stood there. He could sense something was going on. He looked at me confusedly, wondering why I was acting so strange and looking so pale. I pretended I was fine. I wasn't sure what to say. I was trying to blow the whole thing off. I felt so foolish. I was called out because I didn't know how to use a simple metal file. I assumed I had been filing the wrong way. I rubbed the very small file I just found with my hand, trying to figure out which way to use it, secretly, so no one saw me doing it. Was it away from my body? Toward me? I really didn't know. I was too ashamed to ask or admit I didn't know.

Driving home that evening, it all came out. I told Cory the story, and all my anger rose up. I was so ticked, so mad at this guy; the nerve of him coming in and doing that to me, especially in front of all those men. It was the same thing I had felt from men on the paint crew as they would call me out and make me look stupid. I wanted to kick this dude's teeth in. I knew I would be heading back the next day to that same shop, and I'd be around that guy. It fueled me all the more. I was so mad at always being seen as so little. I didn't want to take his abuse. I knew I had to say something to him, confront him.

That evening I had some time on my own because Jayne was working late. I went to a nearby park and started climbing some rocks so I could be alone with God and write in my journal. I made it to an overlook with a good view of the city. I sat there fuming, trying to understand what was happening. Why did I feel so foolish, so mad and angry? *What is so deep about this, God?* I thought. *What am I going to do?*

I sat there, confessing what I felt, talking it out with God aloud on the rocks. Then this thought came to me: *You were in a world of men, working with tools, and you didn't know what you were doing.* As I sat there, the weight of that statement hit something deep inside of me. It was at the core, really my worst fear: being in a world of men, with tools in my hand, and not knowing what I was doing. But I was supposed to. I was a man, wasn't I? A man was supposed to know how to do these things, wasn't he?

It was probably the youngest and most raw I had felt since moving to Colorado. So I sat on the rock and cried. I felt so alone, so boyish, so deeply ashamed for not knowing what to do. Those words penetrated me. It hurt so much to say that, but it was true. It was my deepest fear. Then a fear just as deep surfaced: *As opposed to a man coming over to help me, I will just be called out, exposed. I am all alone to figure it out.*

It was probably one of my deepest fears. *It was all up to me.*

I let out this longing in that desperate place, in the midst of those raw tears. *Father,* I prayed, *would You teach me? Show me how to do this. Don't leave me in this place.* I walked home. I woke up the next day to drive to Denver with Cory. While I was angry before, I had a new peace about it, as if the tears offered me some relief, a release of some pain inside me. As we drove, Cory asked me more about it, and I told him I felt like I was supposed to talk to this guy at the bike shop. We talked it through on our drive.

I went into the bike repair area and got to work. I didn't see him there, so I started sawing. Within a few minutes I noticed the man walk over to his station only a few feet away. My heart rate shot up. There he was. I was trembling just thinking about it, my heart racing with emotion—so much fear, hesitation, and anxiousness. I was starting to think, *It's not that big a deal. Just leave it alone. Don't worry about it. You prayed about it. Things are cool now.* But I knew by my reaction what I was supposed to do.

And so I walked over to his station. I told him in a trembling voice, "Hey, I am so sorry for messing up the file yesterday. Umm … to be honest, I really don't know that much about tools and how to use them, and I would love if you see me doing something wrong today if you'd just come over and show me what I am screwing up." It all came out in one long run-on sentence—no breath. I finished the statement and gulped for air, my muscles still tense. Then I paused and waited. He looked at me, shocked. I looked at him, shocked that I had just said what I had, afraid of what would come next, feeling small and laid bare. We stared at each other for an awkward moment. Then he offered his hand, shook mine, and told me his name. I didn't know how to continue the conversation; I was so nervous, and out of breath, and empty. So I gave him my name and bolted back to my workstation to breathe again.

I had done it. I was so excited. I had just confronted a man with kindness instead of rage. I faced my shame. I confronted my fears. I had even asked him to help. I could have walked out the store and been a very content and happy man. But it was not over. An hour or so later, out of nowhere, the guy came over to my station with a saw in his hand. He approached me and said, "I noticed you working on that metal. I think this saw with the smaller blades might cut it better than the one you have." Was he really over here helping me? Was this the same guy that blew me off yesterday in front of all these guys, giving me a tool and a suggestion? He was here at my workstation, offering his assistance? I tell you, it was the most awkward moment. I couldn't believe what was happening. I was receiving what I had asked for, both from God and from man. I couldn't even shake his hand. I thanked him and took the saw. It was one of the simplest and greatest and most awkward experiences of my life. I didn't make him feel small; I didn't shrink away from his act from the day before. I had faced him. Honored what I really needed. And he had, in turn, come back and given me a tool and his help.

25

ASK

Which of you, if his son asks for bread, will give him a stone? Or if
he asks for a fish, will give him a snake? If you, then, though you are
evil, know how to give good gifts to your children, how much more
will your Father in heaven give good gifts to those who ask him!

Matthew 7:9–11

I had another meeting with my mentor at his office. I was sharing a
bit of my struggles with gear and my need to buy things. He asked,
"What if you prayed and asked the Father for gifts instead of buying
them yourself?" Ask God? It would have been one thing if we were
talking about spiritual gifts or some lofty thing of great significance
in the heavenly realm that would have made sense to pray for. But
we were talking about real physical things that seemed to have no real
significance to the spiritual lives of anyone—including me.

"Really, just gifts?"

I confess I thought of it as a crazy idea for so many reasons. Why would God care about these desires of mine? All this stuff? Look at how many things I had already bought for myself. I had a collection of too many things that started way too long ago as a spoiled kid and was getting me into trouble. It was probably the last thing I needed—more stuff. With all those kids dying in third-world countries for just a bit of food, somehow God was going to send special gifts and His resources to some rich, entitled kid in Colorado? No way. If anything, I needed to sell most of my stuff and turn the check over to the food bank.

It was interesting where my thinking went on this. Because while I never invited God into my purchases, never prayed about my desires and wants and needs in this area, I sure was not afraid to go spend it on myself. It didn't stop me from taking it in my own hands. I never thought of God in any way when I went to these stores. I just saw God as separate from these things. And while I hated buying so much, I kept doing it. Keeping it hidden, like a secret ritual from everyone, especially my wife.

I guess I needed to take care of myself. It was like some form of self-initiation, self-making, and self-soothing to buy my way in. John was saying I should ask someone else for them. *Ask God.* It was hard but good to have him ask me about this. He explained that when his family was broke a few years back, living off a small paycheck, they would often experience amazing gifts from people in all kinds of ways: a vacation or something timely that provided for the family in need. He said now that he has more money, it looks very different, with new challenges, and while he can buy the vacation spots, it's just not the same anymore as it was back then.

It made me wonder: Would God really care about me? To ask God for needs required the hardest part of it all—to wait. And to believe He wanted good things for me. I had to wait and see if He would provide for me. Would I be willing to do that? It meant not getting what I wanted when I wanted it. What if He didn't? I think that is part of why I never invited Him into my decisions: I didn't want to have to risk that. It was easier to just do it on my own.

John asked me, as he saw me wrestling with all this, "Could we pray together? And see if God has any gifts He wants to give you?" I agreed, still a bit confused. We sat there in his office and prayed the most foolish, awkward prayer: for God to give an overstuffed, self-seeking gear guy more gifts. But I prayed. And yes, it is what I wanted. The gifts God had for me. It felt selfish. Egocentric. Prideful. But I prayed, *God, bring Your gifts.*

26

PLACE

The highest heavens belong to the LORD, but
the earth he has given to man.

Psalm 115:16

Until modern times, we focused a great deal of the
best of our thought upon such rituals of return to the
human condition … A man would go or be forced to
go into the wilderness, measure himself against the
Creation, recognize finally his true place within it, and
thus be saved both from pride and from despair.

Wendell Berry, *What Are People For?*

There is, among men, a universal
longing to go back to the earth
from whence they came.

Herbert Roush

The area of wilderness where the Smith family had hunted elk for the past twenty-five years was located on Medino Pass near the Sangre de Cristo Mountain Range. It was ten miles beyond the rural small town of farmers and ranch hands in Westcliffe, Colorado. You drove until the buildings, people, and streets faded and all you had was a simple dirt road that eventually gave way to pure and undisturbed earth. Somewhere hidden in it all was the hope of elk. It was God's country kind of land. Nothing handmade or constructed of steel or concrete, just stretches of pure forest and valleys that extended and stretched in all directions.

It was my first year with them and I wanted to really understand the landscape, since I was to be hunting on it the following year. I wanted to "feel out" the topography of the place, get my bearings. Since there were no markers, no street signs, borders, or boundaries visible, I pulled out my map with man's marks of elevation gains, trail markers, mileage units, and longitudinal coordinates. I took it to Earl, hoping to make sense of it. He looked at me with a smirk, his speckled gray mustache moving slightly, and said, "I've made my own map."

"Briefly, the history of America goes like this: There was a frontier, and then there was no longer a frontier. It all happened rather quickly. There were Indians, then explorers, then settlers, then towns, then cities. Nobody was really paying attention until the moment the wilderness was officially tamed," Elizabeth Gilbert writes in *The Last American Man.*[38]

My suburban experience with land had always been largely constrained to our nicely manicured and mulched one-acre homesite with a littering of a few trees. The true proof of wide-open land in Brentwood was if you could hit and throw a baseball on it. That was open range. And since most homes in the area were being subdivided into smaller quarter-acre tracts, easily mowed with a few swipes of a weed whacker, our acreage, being one acre, felt like wilderness territory fit for pioneers and trappers. While I was somewhat content with being a domesticated Davy Crockett, I always wondered what it would be like to measure myself against storms, unending backwoods trails, and foreign land—land that was not as safe as the paved streets and mulched pathway that looped around our backyard.

I wasn't trying to kid anyone. I knew I had no proven ability to live off land, eating wild berries and hunting squirrels for my survival. I wish I could, but I knew I couldn't. I would have loved to go "into the wild," but I had always been more of a suburban explorer with all my techno gadgets. I confess that I just followed the street signs and my voice-guided GPS like I followed a lot of things into this modern, technological world.

Throughout my years I had traveled to some amazing wilderness areas in California, Oregon, and Hawaii, and been to some remarkably beautiful vacation spots in Italy and France with my family. But it was always by machines of transportation to get to those beautiful places. There was no actual effort or physical energy required. You essentially hopped on and arrived at the places to take pictures.

As Wendell Berry explains:

> With the rise of industry, we began to romanticize the wilderness—which is to say we began to institutionalize it within the concept of the "scenic."

Because of railroads and improved highways, the wilderness was no longer an arduous passage for the traveler, but something to be looked at as grand and beautiful from the high vantages of roadside. We became viewers of "views." And because we no longer traveled in the wilderness ... we transformed the wilderness into scenery, we began to feel in the presence of 'nature' an awe that was increasingly statistical. We would not become appreciators of the Creation until we had taken its measure. Once we had climbed or driven to the mountaintop, we were awed by the view, but it was an awe that we felt compelled to validate or prove by the knowledge of how high we stood and how far we were.[39]

I think that is what made my time with these men so unique. They weren't conquering mountains by statistical measurement and for bragging rights. They were using their feet and bodies to experience and enjoy the land. They were connected to it. They were trying to be more like the land—with their earth-scented wafers and camouflage colors—so they could disappear into its covering.

While it may have looked like I was regressing, going backward in progress and innovation, it actually felt like I was becoming more human rather than less. I was leaving the suburbs, paved roads, and buildings to step back in time. There even seemed a greater appreciation for the earth, God, and creation. As I placed my feet on leaves and rocks, waded into cold mountain streams and sacred hunting grounds, it was as if I was rediscovering these lands for the first time. To just watch the earth rise from a tree stand, which at first seemed such a boring proposition, could make you feel emotions not known. I found myself in midday taking naps in Colorado valleys and waking to watch a bee collect its pollen for twenty minutes. I had never stopped, never looked around or taken the time to see such things.

Edmund Carpenter writes, "The landscape conveys an impression of absolute permanence ... It is simply there—untouched, silent and complete. It is very lonely, yet the absence of all human traces gives you the feeling you understand this land and can take your place in it."[40]

It was all here before. I had been in places like this. But I began to see and experience the land so differently. I was taking part in the landscape, noticing the sounds and sights. Exploring and sneaking around it. I was no longer just a tourist snapping pictures to show at a later date. I had to be present and absorb my surroundings, understand which direction the winds were blowing and what the clouds were doing above. You were required to know the place. Jere was teaching me to turkey hunt, how to blend into the rocks and trees in my camo so as not to spook a turkey. I was becoming connected to it.

Harry Middleton in talking about the old men in his book, *The Earth is Enough*, said, "When you have lived with the land as long as they had, if you're lucky, there comes a point when the land is part of you and you are part of it ... It's in you, all its rich bounty, its pain and loss, like blood and tissue."[41]

It seemed God was raising and initiating me into what it meant to be male, and human, and much of this was by understanding my place, and the earth, and the dirt from which I came. Not by studying it through geography class and a textbook, or in attempts to make money off it, but by experiencing and enjoying it. Learning the meaning of Adam coming up from the dust of the ground by taking my place in it. Feeling its largeness and my smallness by just being in it.

Now when Earl said he had made his own map, what he meant was that he had made this *place* his own. Not using stats and numerical data to guide him, but twenty-five years of traveling all around and about it. He knew it because he had walked it. And yet it was not his land. And that is what fascinated me about Earl, Steve, Charles, Mark, P.J., and Ron, and many others who were taking me out: They seemed to have no desire to possess the lands; they simply enjoyed them.

As I spent time with these men, I heard things like, "I am going to go tomorrow morning and sit right off The Fingers." Or, "I am heading up to Baldy," which was next to Buckskin. These descriptions were not on my government-issued map, not in the portable GPS unit I brought with me or the one suction-cupped in my truck. You couldn't Google or MapQuest Baldy or The Fingers and get a time of arrival and listed direction. In fact, unless you had been hunting with the Smiths, you would have no idea where these places existed. They weren't on maps. It was similar to a secret tribal Indian language known only by these men from the years of hiking through the land and heading to various spots to hunt. You could only decipher the code by experiencing the places. And having the men teach you. They were the maps.

It was so different than the world I had come from where geography was defined for a man "by his house, his office, his commuting route, and the interiors of shopping centers, restaurants, and places of amusement—which is to say his geography is artificial."[42]

On one of my first trips with the Smiths, I asked where these names originated: Buckskin, Moeller, and Baldy; Red Gate, the Zoo, and The Fingers. One of the men, Richard, a man of a few words, simply said, "Some secrets you don't get to learn on the first trip." I felt like I was getting too personal, but then he grinned and said, "I think the cowboys told us those." This brought up another question: Who in the world were the cowboys?

It was the same with Ron. He had named holes up and down the Arkansas River, throughout Eleven Mile Canyon, and on Estes Park's Taylor and Big Thompson rivers during his many years of fishing. Each stretch of river that yielded trout was given a custom name separate from its posted name, if it had one. They were his holes, their names known only to him and those he chose to share them with. They were pockets of water named for reasons he had decided; nothing brilliant, just basic. Some were named because a guy he was fishing with got really lucky there, like the Ryan Hole, the Campbell Hole, and the Meeker Hole. Other names, like Cemetery Hole and Deadwater Hole, describing the land they were near.

Ron knew the holes because of something called memory. They were in his head to mark what had happened. It seemed the same with all the men. I was starting to learn the places, and the names connected to the land, and feeling part of it. And I was starting to see what Wendell Berry meant when he said, "By understanding accurately his proper place in Creation, a man may be made whole."[43]

27

WORDS

For a blessing to be a blessing it must always come
from one who is higher in some felt or real sense:
an older man, a good man, a father figure, one with
the energy of a king, one who has real power, one
who gives what Dad could not or would not give.

Richard Rohr, *Adam's Return*

Your name will no longer be Jacob, but Israel, because you
have struggled with God and with men and have overcome.

Genesis 32:28

I was nearing the end of my painting career. It was my last week
of work, and my boss, Mike, was awarding a stainless-steel grill to
the winner of a contest he'd created. He had told us about it all
summer, flaunting it like a carrot, dangling it in hopes we might

work harder. It was to be awarded to the best painter on the crew and decided by our votes. He assembled the crew—Juan Carlos, Jack, Jesse, John, Carlos, Cory, and me—gathering us in a circle in the parking lot after lunch, right next to his truck with the grill in the bed.

To be frank, I knew I didn't have a shot at the thing. I was nowhere near the skill level of many of the other guys on the crew. As Mike asked us to share who we voted for, there were a bunch of words for Carlos, a few for Jack, and some for John. I knew I was not the best on the crew—but still, something in me longed to be recognized as a hard worker. Just as John finished sharing about his choice of Carlos for his work ethic, Mike said, "Why don't you share who else you wrote down, John?"

It would be helpful to know that in one of my quarrels with John a few months back, I confronted him. He had been critiquing my work again and giving me a hard time. In a sense of frustration and need, I went up to him and simply said, "John, I feel like you are always critical of me. I am not a very good painter. But it would be nice every once in a while if you would just offer some encouragement."

When I looked up at his face, it was expressionless, and he had no words. He just walked away.

As we sat around the grill, our boss waited for John to speak up. He seemed almost caught off guard by it, hesitating, but then spoke from the corner of his mouth: "I also wrote down and wanted to mention Xan for his work at the Weber job site. His caulking lines have really improved."

It was a simple line, barely a compliment to some people. Not spoken with force or even assurance. I didn't win anything. Just improved caulk lines. But it's hard to explain the feelings that went through me, the enormous weight of hearing a man who had given me so much frustration now giving me a compliment. It felt like Simon Cowell on *American Idol* giving me a deeply craved, stunning review. It was the most unexpected surprise.

I think somehow he knew I was dying for it. And that is what felt so kind. He had honored that request; he had given me what he knew I longed to hear. He had blessed me. The man who had given me so much crap, who had wrapped me around shame and struggle, and who I had wished at times would just go away, had just offered words to me the size of Texas. I was beaming. I was trying to hold it in and act calm, but I really wanted to jump on John and hug him.

I left lunch, got in my truck, and drove back to the job site. I tried to keep myself from breaking down as I drove back to work; those words meant so much. It was weird because it was just about caulking, not exactly deeply spiritual or really peering-into-my-soul stuff. I had many a man give me much more insight than that, but maybe nothing with such impact to my heart.

It's hard to really say why. I know I was begging for his approval in some unhealthy ways. But I think it had a lot to do with earning his words, from being with him so, so many days, before they finally came. He wasn't biased, had no real personal interest in me, unlike my dad or maybe a mentor who was going to do his best to encourage me. In fact I don't think John even liked me. But somehow that made the weight of the compliment even greater. Richard Rohr made some sense of this for me:

"Because initiators did not give away privilege, status, and respect cheaply, youth were made to earn them. The same thing happens in the military, sports ... It is tough love, but still love in a way that a male respects and honors—as long as it is not cruel or demeaning. In later years, men largely recall and remember their tough teachers and their demanding coaches, those who pushed them to their best and their limits."[44]

It made me wonder if John the painter was part of my initiation all along. That I did not see over all those berating days, and frustrating moments, and crappy insults because there was something I had to go through. He was hard on me. We had many arguments. I had to face him a few times and let the boy inside of me out and share my needs. But his words at the end are the ones I take with me; they are like gold to me. It meant so much to receive them that still to this day, months later, I find it hard to write this without tears. I think because they came from my experience of him seeing me. The truth is, I hadn't ever spent so much time with men before. This was all day for months. From the time I started the job, I felt a sense of having to earn my place with these men. Respect was not just given away, and I wasn't immediately accepted. I felt like I had to really earn that compliment. And it is probably why it meant so much. Richard Rohr says, "Males need to need and work for male love. Love does not work for the male when it is given away too cheaply, too quickly, or too easily. It turns him into a lazy manipulator instead of a strong man."[45]

I think that is part of my story. I had never had to work for a blessing. It makes sense when I look out at my generation how we can be more of what Rohr explains as the manipulator than the strong man. We are smooth talkers. We can work our way in and out of things. We can persuade well. And I was a king at talking teachers out of late papers and missed tests. In college I was chosen by a finance teacher and taken to a lunch with a wealthy donor for the business school at University of Tennessee. I was sitting around finance majors and highly intelligent students way beyond my gifting, but at the end of the meal, the man was asking about my career and what I was doing outside of school. I was chosen by the teacher because I was good with words, represented myself well. But I knew about ten percent what my peers knew. I saw it as a win that day. I had always prided myself in being able to do this. I was social chairman of my fraternity, then rush chairman. I knew how to recruit guys, convince them to join our fraternity. Won a national award for it. But there wasn't an earned place in it. It was more manipulation and charm. Hollow.

I had always used my white-collar ability to network and make connections. But with these men, none of that worked. You earned your way by proving yourself by way of physical work. And while I hated not being able to charm my way in, talk my way around to getting them to like me, I think I came to be deeply grateful for being in the company based on my work.

It seemed true of the story of Jacob in Scripture. Jacob lives his entire life as a swindler with words. Jacob means "deceiver." He deceives his father to steal his brother's blessing. He grows up near his mother's side. He lives his life as a manipulator. Goes on to create an elaborate scheme to trick his relative, Laban, and steal his prize sheep. But then one day God meets him in the crossing at Jabbok. God doesn't speak words or call out his deception. God doesn't engage him in that way. Instead He physically wrestles with him. It's a new confrontation. And Jacob rises to the occasion, refusing to let go. He is finally met by a stronger man, and there seems a moment where he finally deals with his status and his need of God. He wants a blessing. And God gives it to him, injuring him, then giving him a new name: Israel, "because you have struggled with God and with men and have overcome" (Gen. 32:28). I think that is what I had so little experience in: struggling with men and God for a blessing, being physically tested and having to fight through it.

John couldn't have cared less about my qualifications, that I was an educated man. It didn't earn his, or anyone else's, approval. What did matter to them was what you could put in on the job. John told me I was a horrible painter. And for the most part, I was. I think I needed someone to be honest with me. And that is what made it so powerful in the end. I had earned that compliment, wrestled through my work, not by my charm or sweet-talking mouth. And I think it allowed me to receive his words as a gift of grace.

I left at the end of that week, stepping away from the job of painting. No formal ceremonies. No good-bye wishes. No paper diploma to frame. Nothing but John's words—fresh and lingering, heavy on my heart like a great medallion. I would have never known it, all those times together, but the entire time of that wrestling and struggle was really worth receiving that one line from John. They were hard earned, but a gift from John. Ultimately a gift from God for my labor.

28

GIFT

I long to see you so that I may impart to you
some spiritual gift to make you strong.

Romans 1:11

There were so many memories being made, none greater than fly-fishing the South Platte with Ron, Timm, and Cory in Eleven Mile Canyon. To be wedged between the red canyon walls with these three men, one strong river passing through our legs and around granite boulders, delivering fishing holes ripe for the picking, was true wonder. While we would spread out up and down holes, we were always in sight to see a rod bent and the flash of that iridescent sheen that would inevitably bring a proud whistle from Ron on the river as you reeled in a trout.

Ron and Timm had given Cory and I a few lessons at Ron's cabin on how to tie flies with their jawed metal vises that would hold down the tiny hooks while wrapping peacock feathers, threads, and copper wire together to form what was called a brassie fly. I had never given much consideration to the long and meticulous act required to produce one small fly, but the more trout I caught alongside these men, the more my desire grew for tying my own flies. There was such a sense of satisfaction in catching a trout with a meal of carefully crafted beads and feathers on a tiny hook. I had watched Ron and Timm work diligently on some of the most beautiful flies, and then there were those moments when they stood behind me, guiding my hands and giving me instructions. It should not be surprising if I told you I was ready to buy another piece of gear: a fly vise.

But a fly vise with all the accoutrements was not cheap; at least, not a good, solid, aluminum-and-metal, well-crafted one that would last. Every once in a while I would walk into our fly shop in town, Angler's Covey, and gaze at the fly vises in the glass case like a girl might gaze at a diamond. Normally I would justify a good reason to buy gear. But I found myself on edge, holding back more. I was trying to stop buying so much. And a vise would be a rather expensive purchase. Besides, what would Jayne think? These thoughts would play in my head as I would hold the vise, imagining myself tying up flies. Then I would stop, put it down, and walk away. It was a new experience for me to stare at something I wanted and not get it, to think about it and walk out. But I just couldn't justify this one. It didn't feel right.

But I kept going back, walking in, looking around at the Patagonia jackets, Simms waders, the fly selections, then heading over to stare into the glass cases and wrestling with my desire only to walk away again. I was having a harder time justifying it—not as easily as it was before. I must have gone in four or five times looking at it, each time getting a bit closer to diving in and making the reckless purchase. But always backing off. And trying to be patient.

A few months later I was coming down from a weekend retreat in the mountains with two friends, David and Gus, from Tennessee. David asked me, "Is there a fly shop on our way back into town?" I explained there was and he said he wanted to stop by. As we were driving, I began to wonder why he wanted to go. What did he need? It was unusual the way he asked. I waited awhile, then asked, "Why do you want to go?"

"I want to buy a fly vise."

We both sat there for a while. Then he interrupted the silence, putting more meaning to his statement. "It's for you, Xan. God told me to buy it for you."

Okay. This was really weird to hear. It did not seem like a random coincidence. My first thought was that I must have told him at some point I wanted the vise. But he said that he had no idea I wanted one. I was just really puzzled, still trying to make sense of it all. David looked at me and said, "You helped me understand more of myself this weekend. The Lord wants me to buy you a fly vise as a gift."

A gift? A fly vise? The Lord?

I know this story seems so cliché—I asked; God brought a vise. Isn't God great? If you recall, my mentor had said I should pray for gifts. And while I had plans to, I never really got around to doing the actual formal praying for a vise. It still felt too selfish. I didn't know if God was even listening or watching. I saw this more as my fatal addiction. And yet I really did wait. And I really did want it.

We walked into the fly shop and David said, "Which one have you been looking at?" And I felt like a jerk. I wanted to point to the cheapest one, but it was not the one I was looking at each time I went. He asked again: "Which one do you want?" I was fighting back the urge to tell him, "No. This is the last thing I need. I've got enough gear in my garage. Let's get out of here, maybe give some money to the homeless."

But it was just a really confusing and profound moment for me. I did want one. But I was stuck between my desire and my shame of thinking I didn't deserve it. While buying it on my own was always self-indulgent and produced shame, this was about being given a gift from David and God. I was not sure if I was open to receive that thought.

I could not help but see this was not just one event, but many that were happening. Similar to losing my bags on my hunting trip to Nashville, and many other moments seeing God provide in my marriage, or with finances. And while it was not immediate, not over one thing, I began to sense something slowly growing in me: the idea that I had a Father who cared for me. A Father who saw me. A Father who could give me gifts if He wanted to. Maybe I didn't have to take care of myself and watch out for my own self-interest all the time. Maybe I just needed to ask.

It was a fly vise, but it became a symbol that God really saw me. He saw me waiting, watching, hesitating. And not only that, but He cared for my desires, the simple pleasure of having a vise. I don't think I knew God cared that much or in that way; maybe I knew it but I didn't believe it. I remembered John's words: "Stop. Let others do it. Let God give you gifts."

I always thought God would want to meet me at some deep spiritual level, a coming through of great, holy magnitude. But this experience made me wonder if I needed to learn to trust Him at this level, a basic level. Jesus appears to His disciples after the crucifixion, and as a sign, He sends them a net full of fish. "What was so spiritual about that?" you might ask. It seemed to speak to their place of deep desire and connection with their way of life, of what they had been in search of, and how He had met them before, much like my reconnection to God by these ways as well. The fly vise was a sign that God cared—He saw me. That it was Jesus.

I think David's gift freed some locked places in me to care for others and not spend as much time looking after myself and buying shiny new stuff. Because if God saw my needs, even my desires, then maybe I didn't have to spend so much time worrying about collecting it on my own. Maybe He could bring me good gifts.

29

MEASURE

A giant nearly ten feet tall stepped out from the Philistine line into the open, Goliath from Gath. He had a bronze helmet on his head and was dressed in armor—126 pounds of it! He wore bronze shin guards and carried a bronze sword. His spear was like a fence rail—the spear tip alone weighed over fifteen pounds.

1 Samuel 17:4–7 MSG

The weight of a fish is commonly its only title to fame.

Henry David Thoreau

Ron's personal record for the amount of trout caught on his fly line in a single day was one hundred. His biggest trout was a rainbow that weighed in at six and a half pounds and stretched out at twenty-eight inches long. But what I was learning about Ron is that math was not calculated through accurate empirical and statistical measuring;

I never saw a scale or measuring tape in his vest. Ron's count and size were mere estimations, guesses. But not educated guesses; more like larger-than-life projections of what he wanted them to be, stories that turned into tales that told a few more times stretched into legendary Ron proportions, much like the man himself.

I know this because one day at Rosemont Lake the fishing was hot, the kind you might only get once a year. Trout were rising on mayfly hatches and making ripples across the lake like a rainstorm. I had twelve rainbows and two cutthroat trout by lunch break and was feeling very proud. I was hoping to out-do my fishing guru, Ron, and was keeping a close tally with my eyes from the other side of the lake. From my record we had been matching trout for trout. But as we gathered for lunch, I told him mine, and his number was suddenly thirty. And when I pressed him, he admitted he didn't actually keep count.

I can remember walking into outdoor sports stores as a younger man, seeing men on corkboards, displaying their trophy fish, turkey, or deer—proudly holding their fresh kill. It was laughable to me. What were they trying to prove? Hundreds of pictures posted like a wall of desperate missing children in search of someone to love them. Or tell them they were a real man. I always thought that was so foolish, so redneck, and ridiculous.

Who would want to do that?

It only took my first trout and seeing P.J.'s bull elk with its antlers spread out in all directions to begin the quest every hunter and fisherman inevitably begins: to enter this cycle of record keeping and storytelling. Purchasing a measuring tape. And wanting a trophy and a story to tell.

Jere, the banker and big trophy hunter, was not asking how beautiful the colors were, or about the setting sun, or "How do you feel?" Jere, like so many men, would ask the question, "How big was it?" What did it weigh? How many points on its antlers? What was the trout's length? What did the antler's rack score on Boone and Crockett? A whole system of measurements based on the rack's thickness, length, and antler extensions are calculated for its accurate point value. A 350 bull was a nice one. A 250? Well, kind of small. A man had a need to know—size really mattered.

It seemed that to understand a man's true worth, you had to figure out his score and measure him. As one wealthy man I met confessed, "Money is how I now keep score."

I had thought I was very well beyond and above all of this non-spiritual and nonsensical comparing mumbo jumbo. This was for the competitive, carrot-chasing fools. But within a few months of catching trout, I was documenting my fish in pictures, and had learned some of the basic techniques of making a fish look larger by extending the elbows and pushing your fish into the camera while you moved away from the picture to the back—a classic way of making anything big. I then put them on my version of the corkboard wall: Facebook.

I knew better. I knew this was not the true answer or reason I was here. It was about the men and the experience. But I couldn't help it. Size and weight seemed to matter. Even looking at the story of David and Goliath, you know a man was giving the account. A woman would have just left it with descriptions like "a really big monster," but a man needed more of the detail. According to 1 Samuel 17, Goliath was over nine feet tall and wore a bronze coat of armor that weighed about one hundred and twenty-five pounds; his spear's iron point weighed about fifteen pounds.

Notice all the measurements? Now, I am not saying he was lying about it or stretching the truth, but his height is debated amongst scholars and different texts have him ranging from six-foot-seven to nine-foot-six tall. And the reason? My guess is because men were telling the story, and as the story was told, Goliath got bigger and bigger, much like Ron's fishing tales.

And why do you think no one wanted to fight Goliath? It was simple. They measured themselves, and simply put, they came up short.

It would be easy to dismiss this, realizing what David did with his sling of faith, showing man has no need to measure. Of course. I agree. God looks at the heart, not the outward appearance. The story proves it. And I believe that is true. But I also believe that we don't just get there on our own; most of us have to enter a process to get there (even David had killed lions and bears first). It was a cycle moving from one to another. A friend, Dave Leinweber, who owns the largest fly shop west of the Mississippi, (oops, did I just measure again?), explained it this way:

> When folks begin to fish, all they can think about is catching that first fish. Then as soon as they catch that first fish, they have to catch another. Then it becomes about how many fish, and I caught twenty or forty or eighty fish! Then it becomes about how big and catching that twenty-plus inch fish, then the twenty-five-plus then the

thirty-plus ... Then it becomes about the exotic, either fishing in some exotic place or catching something unique. Then there seems to be a shift and it becomes more about the fishing and less about the fish. You get out and catch a fish just to prove that you still have what it takes. The final stage has very little to do with the fish other than they are there. Catching is just a bonus. Fishing becomes larger than any fish and more than any quantity. Being out with the smells, sights, and sounds is all that becomes important. A time to renew the soul and hear God's voice.[46]

It was so true. It made me think of my grandfather. He died when I was twelve. But as a four-year-old boy I remember heading out to lakes to fish for bass and bluegill. We would sit on lakeshores, and he would put worms on the hook that my little arms were too small to grab, and I would cast out. I kept hooking them on, one after another, something like twenty or thirty in one day. My grand-father rarely went fishing anymore. It was as if my grandfather had made it through that process. He had done it all, but here he was fishing with his grandson, and here I was so busy at catching them that I was unable to see it for what it was. Maybe that was the beauty of it all. It was part of that journey. I didn't know all of that because I wasn't a father yet; I was simply a son.

It made me wonder about all those pictures of men with their trophy kills: bears, sheep, elk, and deer. Who was with them? Who was behind the camera taking the picture? Maybe an older man who helped them make the kill—a man who knows it has nothing to do with the picture or the trophy and everything to do with being in nature and the renewal of the soul. A man who obliges because he knows the younger man still needs the picture, the stories, the measurements.

I won't lie: I was right in the middle of it. And yet it seemed there was a time to be part of that. It was a snapshot of the journey of a man. I think that's why even though I knew of the process, I still found myself secretly trying to catch more fish than Timm or Cory. And bigger ones. Still posting my pictures on my Facebook account. I felt so stupid. I just imagined the people looking at it and laughing. Laughing like I did at all those boards at outdoor and hunting stores. Here I was—now I was the joke. But somewhere between reading what Dave said and understanding that cycle for myself, I was okay with it. I was a young man trying to make my way through it.

It hit me that maybe the great tragedy of these sports is when men get stuck, unable to graduate to that next stage of maturity, wisdom, and the simple enjoyment of nature. It saddens me when I see older men continue to pursue trophy catches. Even the great naturalist and Christian John Muir believed hunting was an adolescent instinct that was meant to lessen with age.

It all came full circle one day on the Big Thompson in Estes Park. It was a magical day of blue skies and bountiful trout with my fishing mentor, Ron. At one point while we were resting, Ron grabbed me on the shoulder and said, "You have to promise me one thing. That one day, when I am really, really old and can't move my legs, that you will come find me at an old folks home, take me in my wheelchair onto this river, and let me fly-fish."

I was beginning to feel the great mystery of these waters and the great invitation of these men moving me into deeper stages—and, maybe the greatest compliment and invitation of all, I would in turn be part of some of their final moments on this earth. I was humbled by Ron's request. I told Ron yes. I would be honored. And I would also be closely watching his fish count.

30

FATHER

Lying on our backs in the parking lot, staring up at the
one star that came through the streetlights, I asked
Tyler what he'd been fighting. Tyler said, his father.

Fight Club

When you are a young man, you see what your father is not.

Richard Rohr

My friend and elk-hunting buddy, P.J., was becoming a real hero
to me. Some of this was because of what he had been through as
a boy and the risks he had taken in starting a new business despite
some saying he was not up for the challenge. P.J. came from a hardworking coal mining town in West Virginia where money was hard
to find, but risks were easy to spot, usually due to the influence of
alcohol. He had grown up with the values that tough, backbreaking

work instills, with plenty of visible suffering, and at times poverty—
including food stamps. I believe the growing gift of our friendship
was in our differences, that we had come from very polar-opposite
backgrounds and lessons from them. One example: P.J. hoarded and
was disciplined; I was carefree, more extravagant, full of risk. But
these seemed to draw us together.

One day I told him how my father took my brother and me
to his stockbroker to purchase stocks when we were teenagers. P.J.
was floored: "What? Are you serious? My dad never taught me anything about business or investing. I wish he had." While he had been
schooled in the outdoors, even given off a school day for opening
deer season, there wasn't any instruction on the business side.

P.J. and I bonded through time spent in the woods hunting elk
and over conversations about his personal fitness training business.
As I listened, it was interesting to discover how much advice I had
when talking to him. I understood some of the financial issues of his
business, often giving him counsel or strategy, ideas on expanding
that had never crossed his mind. As he taught me about elk, I taught
him a little about business. He was intrigued by my knowledge and
understanding, while I found it rather peculiar to see it as something
valuable, this businessman part of me that I had buried or left somewhere in my rearview mirror.

I began hearing the general theme of P.J.'s story more and more.
Sam, another friend whose father was a home builder, brought him
to his job site and had worked with him over a summer, schooling
him in the craft of building. But he also confessed his father had
never taught or instructed him about the financial side of life; he had
to learn it on his own. It was the same with so many of my friends

in Colorado. Many of their blue-collar dads had given them experiences in the wilderness or under car hoods but had done little the side of business or money. Or advice in careers.

I began to rethink my father. It's still going on today, but it started then. My dad had schooled me as a boy in the world of stocks, spreadsheets, and business plans. He had sacrificed to bring home a computer at a time when few people had one. He taught me how to use a spreadsheet before Excel even existed, back when the monitor screens were green. My hobby in those days was collecting baseball cards, so I organized them by pushing spreadsheets and creating calculation formulas using the *Beckett Monthly Magazine* to figure out card values. I plugged them in like they were NYSE stocks to determine values of my net worth.

My father would drive me to hotels for baseball-card conventions, where I would set up as the youngest vendor with my card displays in the middle of middle-aged men with potbellies staring with confused looks at this kid. My dad talked with one of his vendors and got AutoCAD, a computer design program for architects, because I was interested in going to school for it, and he had shown me how to take risks because he had modeled and lived it. Many of these skills I had picked up and learned from my entrepreneurial dad, who had started a company and eventually sold it for a few million dollars. He helped me compose a business plan for a lawn-mowing company at fourteen and took me down to speak with a bank officer so I could get a loan for a new three-thousand-dollar commercial lawn mower.

For a book about fathering and initiation and the world of men, it is a bit unusual, I admit, to be coming around to my dad here at the end. A little late, right? Actually the timing might be right. I haven't talked much about my dad in this book. To be honest, I hadn't been around him for a while when I was writing it. I moved to Colorado, in some ways, to leave my past, the South, my academic settings, and explore new possibilities out West. I think I wanted to flee my experiences of business Brentwood; in some ways, my father, too. I checked those bags and in time, shed my Polo clothes and all those many things attached to my previous life to emerge a new man out here in new outfits and lifestyle and beliefs. And I was pretty okay with that; it seemed to be where God was leading me—at least for a while.

But all of a sudden this part of my life, while forgotten and buried, kept reaching out. I had found myself in very far extremes—polar extremes. I wasn't living in a shanty begging for potatoes on the streets with Jayne, but for me, it felt very far from the manicured living I'd known, like the distance from Tennessee to Colorado was similar to the distance of how far I had travelled in my heart, to the other side of life and masculinity. It would show up on my return trips to Nashville while visiting Brentwood to see my parents for holidays. I would look around at the people, the buildings, the pace of life, the streets I drove as a teenager, the men in suits talking business over lunch; all I could do was stare. I was so taken aback and confused by this world that used to feel so comfortable, familiar, and normal. It now felt strange and awkward, like a foreign traveler might feel in a new city—yet true to some deep place inside me. But it wasn't home anymore. Not familiar. I was even struggling to relate to my friends Matthew and Wade, who were living in Nashville and in business.

There were so many sobering questions I had to wrestle with. *Why was I really doing this? Was this an authentic search for God and myself? Or just some spiritual escapade playing cowboys and Indians in the Wild West? Was I simply running from my father? Was I trying to be the man my father wasn't? Or even trying to overcompensate for the things I did not receive from my life as a privileged kid?* It was tough to understand, complicated to see what God was doing. But there was a shift. A new thing was happening.

The more I thought about all this, the more images of my father kept surfacing. My dad had offered his own take on raising me. While we never went into the woods or scouted elk in high mountain ranges with Earl or Woody, he had ensured our family saw many unique places, even taking my brother and I golfing in Scotland at the legendary St. Andrews golf course, where golf began.

If I was honest, even the city I had so many struggles with had taken me in as a teenager and fathered me in a unique way. An architecture firm in the center of downtown Nashville had started a program for interested young architects. I was shown the ropes by a few of their guys, and even interned for the owners: Gary Everton, Bob Oglesby, and Jerry Askew, of EOA Architects. They took me to lunches, gave me time in their offices, and put me to work, letting me design a few small projects on their personal computers. At the end of my time, there they invited me to play golf with them for their annual gathering. I was trading golf shots with some of the premier architects in town. Another man, Cal, one of the most successful and wealthiest men in Nashville, had spent time over meals and workouts mentoring me about areas of life. He was the owner and CEO of the family-owned Dollar General stores. He had never picked up a fly rod or a shotgun, but he had spent time investing in the person I was becoming, gave words to help me believe my life had meaning and importance.

It was like, "Oh yeah. I forgot about all that." All these memories had been clouded in my western pursuit of what it meant to be male and rugged and tested; I had blocked them out. But thinking back on those men and those experiences, I could see it was very significant; being in a world of stockbrokers, bank officers, CEOs, and architects was like initiation. Initiation in a white-collar setting; it was a little different, not as many mustaches or dirty jeans, but with the same sense of growing me and expanding a vision for my life.

Was all this a worthless pursuit? A long waste of time? Just the prodigal leaving for a far land, someday to return to his homeland? No, I knew God was here. There were significant things that neither Brentwood nor my father could teach me. It made me wonder if somehow we needed both. The city, and office parks, and gentlemanlike things, how to clean up and wear a bow tie, and select fine wine. But also how to walk into the wilderness, cast in the wind, and kill your own meal. While it wasn't about obtaining it all, or being complete, they each had a piece of what it meant to be male, to be a man.

God was raising me, growing me up. Filling in some gaps.

I had heard that a man usually did two things with his father. He either became the face of the enemy, in which all of life's struggles and frustrations and problems were projected, forever blaming and subjecting his father to some impossible scrutiny. Or he made him into a great hero, so perfect that he would spend the rest of his life striving toward that perfect image while knowing inside he will never be able to live up to it. I never would have tried to do this on purpose, but it seemed this quest was about going away into a far land, finding the things I needed that my father could not give me.

Sharon Hersh, a friend and Christian professor in Denver, says that hatred of your father is ultimately hatred of yourself. You cannot hate your mother or your father without hating that part of yourself. I was slowly beginning to see that what I needed most was compassion for those parts of my father just like I needed compassion and grace for myself. I wasn't perfect. He wasn't either. He wasn't the enemy or the hero; he was a man, much like me, with a story and pains and struggles, and a broken relationship with his father too. I had written him off and then gone off to demand that need be met by other men. I had found some other men, but I had left my father behind.

This seemed true of so many men I have met, like some great pandemic across our nation. Fathers and sons so separated. Young men believing the lie that our lives are so different from our fathers'. I think I found some truth when my father gave me a scrapbook as a Christmas gift one year. In it was a picture of three generations of Hoods who had been cutting down trees and making their livelihood in the lumber sawmill business.

I looked at the picture of those Hoods and thought about my father's break from that. It seemed so drastic. Three generations of Hoods who were in pictures all working under one roof, learning the techniques and instructions from the previous generation. They learned from their fathers. Passed it on. But all of that soon changed.

My dad had sent me a saw the same year as the scrapbook. It was a saw I had asked for as a gift. The saw held a central place in the family picture of the three generations; it felt like an image I wanted to carry on. I didn't know exactly why I wanted it, I just did. My father had it in his corporate headquarters office, above his desk.

My father sent this letter with the saw:

> As the years passed of course, your Great Grandpa and Grandpa Hood modernized the operations even more. A gasoline-powered mill was purchased. Motorized chain saws replaced the crosscut saw. Tractors pulled the logs into the mill instead of horses. Fewer men were required to operate the mill compared to the steam engine mill of the past. It is surprising really how few years it took to completely change the operations of the mill and the human labor power it required. I guess that is why the crosscut saw means so much to us. It represents another era—a time when men had to labor together and in this case, on two opposite sides of a manually operated saw. Our forefathers held those handles as they worked to provide a living for their families.

The irony was that in just a short while, everything had changed. What most men did for centuries, farming and mainly physical jobs that were passed down over dozens of generations, had changed in roughly one or two generations. Life was drastically different. With technology, and new industry, our lives were drastically different. Maybe more than any generation before us. It seemed part of what this generation was dealing with. In just a few years our way of life had changed so drastically, so quickly, unlike any in the history of the world. Our grandfathers can't even relate anymore. Life is so different. But it wasn't that way for them or their grandfathers, not such a quick shift.

I think that is what broke the link. We didn't need men on both sides anymore. Three generations of Hoods, all doing the same thing, were broken. My dad found a new opportunity. My dad, like so many in his generation, broke the chain. He went to college, got an MBA, and went from the hardworking life of physical labor to the business world in corporate offices. My grandfather was proud, but he had little to teach my father in this world of business.

In a strange way, many of the things my grandfather loved, I was doing out in Colorado. But my dad, as a young man, had gone in the opposite direction. He left the blue-collar world of his father to enter business, while I was leaving the world of business for this other side. I could not help but feel the divide. Parts of me were in both worlds, yet feeling so far from one another. Each side claiming a few parts and so disconnected from the other.

Our fathers had come from a generation familiar with suffering, hardship, world wars, and depression. Our fathers grew up with their fathers teaching them life lessons. They took them and went on to the business world. They worked hard and hoped in some way to keep their families from that previous life, all the scraping by and suffering. They gave us the good life without the suffering and hardship.

It made me realize that my dad had offered his form of initiation by the way he had experienced life: as a businessman. He was not able to help me catch fish like Ron, or shoot a gun like Charles, Mark, and Steve, but what he could offer, he did. And he didn't necessarily do it knowing why, or how, or under some heading called "initiation." He taught the skills a man needed from what he knew, what he had been taught along the way. I had never interpreted that way. But I began to see how it was true, moments of my childhood where he was there, teaching, offering, fathering.

I discovered I had been given parts of a man, as a boy by my father, and then a much larger community of men had offered more in areas that he could not. It wasn't that one was better than the other, but both were needed. And God had orchestrated both in His own way. There was a need for both. Business. And wilderness.

It made me believe that maybe I had learned a few valuable things from my background and even from my father. Maybe there *was* some form of initiation happening in another setting with men. Not as much with physical dirt, and blood, but with business plans, and stock portfolios, and spreadsheets. I had never seen initiation this way. But it was true. I was as much a businessman as I was a hunter. Maybe that was what was happening out here; God was balancing me out. Drawing me into two sides. The mercy and the strength.

It seemed by being out here, I was actually starting to appreciate my father more. The things he gave me that I never knew were gifts till I was taken from them.

🝆

We were sitting at Christmas together when I leaned over and gave my father my thoughts. I knew there was a bit of a tension in taking this new path, but I leaned in close and told him thank you for what he had given me as a father. He looked at me a little awkwardly, and smiled. That was all, and for that moment, that was enough. I believe something in that moment was healed, restored. I gave dignity and weight to his initiation of me, the only kind he could offer. It felt true. It felt good.

EXIT

DEER

Get your weapons—your quiver and bow—and go out
to the open country to hunt some wild game for me.

Genesis 27:3

Even though I was but a boy, I knew standing there in the
stream that, from then on, things would be different. It was
not that the world had changed, but that I had changed in
some fundamental way that I could not understand or undo.
I felt, too, a sense of actually becoming, belonging.

Harry Middleton, *The Earth Is Enough*

It was an early Sunday morning in Nashville, the rows of churches
still waiting to greet their hungry hosts of people at the 8 and 10
a.m. services. I had been one of them as a boy. But this time I
was hoping to meet God in a different way. Not in an itchy sports

jacket, but in camouflage and in the boondock. I was eager to see what the day's story would be. My wife was would help me understand its meaning.

Cory and I had arrived a few days before. My high school friend and college roommate, Jeremy, and his dad, Jere, had told us to bring our rifles for opening deer season. I had been hunting for a few years now, and I still had not killed any four-legged beast. It was a bit frustrating. I was learning so much, enjoying being in the presence of men and discovering new areas of land, but I was starting to wonder if I was ready to "kill one." Jere had called me out months before; his strategy in hunting and life was, "You have to want it." Jere believes if you are not aggressive and motivated, you will miss the opportunities of life. He backed that up. He hunted and lived that way. As he would listen to some of my pontifications and philosophies on hunting, he would often interrupt and say, "I am questioning if you want it enough, Xan."

I talked more than I acted. It was true.

While I wanted meat, I didn't necessarily need it for survival. It would be great if I got a large animal, but I was willing to wait. *Maybe I'm not being aggressive enough,* I thought. Then again, I didn't want to become some crazy hunter collecting trophies of every animal across the globe. I wanted hunting to be more than just hunting. I wanted fathering and God. I wanted to experience God in these places. But I wondered if Jere was right. Maybe I needed to want it more.

We woke up that morning to darkness. And like every other time, I had forgotten a few items. I ended up wearing Mike's thermal underwear and some gloves from Jere along with my camo pants and shirt. We walked past the front field and into the hunting grounds. We emerged into the large, wide-open field while it was still dark, though the dawn was slowly breaking.

Jeremy walked with me, and we found the double-tree stand at the edge of the field. I was tired, almost exhausted, somewhat unsure of even wanting to be there. We climbed up, hoisted our guns, and sat there together in the dark like two grade-school boys squeezed together in a small undersized desk and chairs, the steel of the stand pressing into our legs and butts as we shifted to stay warm. A few minutes passed, then a few more as the sunrise greeted us. Suddenly we heard a shot. It was in the direction of where our buddy Graham was hunting. I would later learn our longtime fraternity brother had just killed his first buck a few fields away. Jeremy left our stand to go find Graham, which left me there by myself. I sat there in the cold, trying to watch and wait, wondering when my time would come.

Looking back, the significance of being left alone in the field seemed important. I had so many voices over the past few years guiding me, men who had offered their tips, stories, joking, and teasing—and invitations to their wild-game nights. All these voices were there with me in that stand. For so long I had felt like a stranger in this world. But I was one of them now, and the time had come to rely on what those men taught me. This was my time. No more instructions or leaning on others. When Jeremy left the stand, it was like God saying, *Now you are ready. It's just Me and you.*

But I started to get tired. And bored. And cold. I began shifting my body back and forth to stay warm and awake. I would nod off, then pop up and collect myself, then look around and nod off again. Was this my time? Would it happen today? My feelings were an odd mixture of desire and anticipated disappointment. Not a minute later a buck skirted across the field in the now rising sun, glowing and moving like the first deer might have with Adam in the garden. He was probably two hundred and fifty yards out, too far and moving too fast across the meadow for me to scope. There it went again: my chance, my shot. I could hear Jere's voice: "You don't want it enough." I nodded off again.

But then I looked up to see two small deer wandering, almost tiptoeing, down a path about fifty yards away. They were close enough, right in front of me, to take a shot. I grabbed my gun and brought the scope to my eye. I remember for the first time thinking, *Here we go. This might actually happen. I might kill this.*

I noticed through my scope the deer were small, really small. Not babies, but there was no rack. They were probably does. So no big buck to mount on the wall or put on Facebook or on the board at some hunting store. But it seemed fitting for my first: a small doe. Nothing massively special, but enough to pull the trigger on and enter into a new season as a hunter.

I collected myself and lined her up, keeping the gun steady on the metal rest. I breathed slowly out as I was taught and focused my scope right on the lungs, lining up the crosshairs. It all went down so perfectly textbook, just like I had been told. They froze. I shot. It felt so surreal. I had always worried so much about the recoil, "the kick." But I watched right through my scope as the deer dropped to the ground like a brick, falling just below the grass and out of sight.

The other deer froze, confused as to what just happened. Then it hit me. I could take another shot and drop the other deer. I paused for a moment and realized one was enough. One step at a time. Just appreciate this little one, this gift. I was happy, content. I made some noise and revealed myself to scare the other deer off.

Then silence. I didn't quite know what to think. *What have I done? Did I just do that? Is it dead? Did I just kill my first deer? Should I stay in the stand or go over to it?*

Then came an intensive flurry of adrenaline and emotion. The first thing I wanted to do was hug someone or something. I had watched these hunting videos where the men acted like children, hugging each other and crying and carrying on. And while it seemed so foolish at the time, I wanted to celebrate and do all those weird things hunters do when they get an animal. It all came flooding in. I wanted to do all that. But there was no one there. I decided to approach her on my own.

I walked through the grassy field in sober reflection, as if I was about to receive communion, to the spot where I saw the deer drop. I found her, and indeed, she was dead. I had killed a deer. I was ecstatic but sobered. I felt like I'd arrived on the scene of a car crash. There was tragedy on the ground. Life and death. Hope and darkness. And then a tremendous sadness that came over me. I sat over it and prayed as Jere does after every kill. It felt holy: just me and the deer and the mystery of it all.

As the moments passed, I ran my hand across its sides and moved my fingers through the fur. She was warm but limp. Thinking about my plans to field-dress the doe, I moved her legs around and noticed a scrotum. Hold on. She was a he; a buck, not a doe. I looked for the antler spikes, and there they were: tiny knobs just under the hair. Not yet exposed, but poised to emerge.

All of a sudden the symbol was there for me: something young, small, still waiting to emerge and grow. All the parts of me that I had struggled through while feeling like such a boy in a man's world of big bucks. I never removed my hand, pressing it against his side—even moving my hand to his head. The story of Abraham and Isaac flashed to my mind. God taking a young ram in place of Isaac. The sacrifice. Atonement. Replacing his son for the young bull. Atoning for him. The blood sacrifice. It was just a story locked away inside me, but randomly came out in the moment. Was God speaking through it? As I held my hand on his head, much as I imagined the priests of long ago, his warm fur pressed into my hand, this young buck felt like me, in some way.

I held my hand there. Resting. Wondering.

It sounds crazy, but I felt as if there was some transference of one life for another. I was him; he was me. One young buck for another. I felt the weight of the moment, the weight of having killed my first animal, the weight of the animal's sacrifice. I cried real tears, not manufactured ones. I felt the significance and weight of this moment. God being here. My first deer. My story. My connection to this animal. God saying something through it. And I had tears. Good, holy, clean tears.

A few minutes later Jeremy and Graham walked up. Jeremy was wide-eyed. We hugged like old men with strong grips. They were so excited for me. I got the celebratory hugs and screams. Graham shared the story of his eight-point buck he killed a few minutes before. I was so glad for him: ten years hunting to get a deer that size. And then, right as we stood over the deer, we looked up, and another buck, this one a nice-sized eight-point buck, was heading towards us. It was so unusual. We were talking, right downwind of him, easy to see and to smell. I was confused. Jeremy told us to get down. We couldn't figure it out. I thought he would see us and run off, but he was coming closer. Fifty yards. Forty yards. Jeremy said, "Xan, shoot it."

I was still in shock.

"Xan, shoot it."

What? I thought. I will be honest. I didn't want to. I just wanted to appreciate this little guy. It felt like enough. I had my moment with God. I had cried. This was my story and my buck to take away. I was done. It was a settled place for me. I had my first deer and I just wanted to enjoy it. Another deer? That would be like an overstuffed person going up for more pizza at the buffet line. I was full.

I passed on the other deer earlier because I thought it wasn't right, and yet this deer kept coming toward us. Jeremy was still saying, "Xan, shoot it." I was asking, "Jeremy, are you sure I should shoot?" But he couldn't hear because he was bracing for the shot with his fingers in his ears. "Are you sure?" Nothing. The deer was heading right for us. Thirty yards. Now twenty.

A deer is best shot from the side, where you can hit his body, hit his heart, and double-lung him. But he was heading straight for us, not stopping or moving to the side. I was going to have to shoot a moving target and from the front. I had never pictured that. "Jeremy, should I shoot?" Silence. And in one of the most unusual, confusing moments, standing right next to my little buck, I knelt down, raised the rifle, and shot the eight-point buck from the front just as he was closing in. He dropped in the grass like the first one.

This was insane.

The guys around me screamed even louder this time. Jere and Cory rushed in from the other field as I stood over my second deer. And this one was actually a good-sized buck: eight points with a nice basket, a decent trophy. *Why?* I kept wondering. *What's happening to me?* I had spent three years and dozens of days in the woods looking for a deer. Now instead of one, I had two—and I'd shot them within minutes of each other.

I didn't know what to make of it. Two deer. Not a bad morning for a hunter. But it had nothing to do with my skills. The buck was literally going to run into us. I am not kidding. He would have run me over if I hadn't shot him. I didn't understand it. *Why two, God?*

What did it mean? What was this all about? Why would God do this?

I thought I understood about the first deer, but this second one—it didn't make any sense. It felt so wrong to shoot it.

It would soon make sense.

My wife flew in the next day to spend time with my family and me. After leaving the airport, we stopped to talk in, of all places, a Home Depot parking lot. We were catching up, and I was telling Jayne how alone I felt being back in my hometown and how I was struggling with some of the same issues I'd struggled with during my youth. I told her how I was feeling like a disappointment to some family and friends. We prayed. As I looked up, she had tears for me. She felt my pain.

I then realized I had yet to tell her about my hunting trip. I started telling her the story of the first deer. I went through all the details, and midway through she looked at me and, referencing the young buck, assuredly said, "The boy had to die."

I paused to reflect. Her interpretation differed so greatly from mine. I saw the first little buck as me. The young buck. But as she put words to her interpretation, my eyes were opened, and God revealed the mystery of the second deer. If the first was the death of that young, boyish part of my heart, then the second was ...

I sat there and pictured the moment. I remembered a story told by Gordon Dalbey in *Healing the Masculine Soul*. A man has a recurring dream of a lion running toward him. Each time he wakes up frightened to death. Then Gordon tells him to ask who the lion is next time he has the dream. When the man does, the lion replies, "I am you." He had been running from himself. It was all being unveiled there with my wife, and I was caught off guard. I knew that the big buck was never supposed to be in that field moving towards us. Even Jeremy confessed he had never seen anything like it. I pictured again its strength, its full frame moving as if it would walk right into me. I tried to voice my feelings to Jayne: "The buck, it was coming toward me, Jayne. I think it was the part of me that I had never embraced. An eight-point buck. A man. Not a small little buck, though I felt like one. God was sending another buck down the path into me."

"Xan, that buck is you," Jayne said.

Overwhelmed, I sunk into my seat. After so many years of searching, my wife had revealed to me the mystery I could not see on my own. I wonder if God now saw me as a man too. I wept for the first time with my wife in Brentwood at a Home Depot parking lot. This buck was the greatest gift—a gift sent by God to show me who I was and how He saw me. I looked up at her and laughed. "Jayne, we are crying over a deer. A deer!" She smiled with tears in her eyes. And we laughed together.

I guess there are two ways we can find our home. We can stay at home surrounded by its comforts and never leave. Or we can leave only to eventually return.

Jayne looked at me and said, "You do know God had to bring you back here, right here in Nashville, right outside of Brentwood, to do this, right?"

I could only offer more tears knowing that God, my Father, was orchestrating all of this.

I related to Harry in *The Earth Is Enough:* "I knew standing there … that, from then on, things would be different. It was not that the world had changed, but that I had changed in some fundamental way that I could not understand or undo. I felt, too, a sense of actually becoming, belonging."[47]

I felt that I was somehow part of it now. The sweat, blood, and tears. The rituals and the gathering of men.

I think in some way I had returned home.

Home to God. Home to Brentwood. Home to myself, now a man.

Notes

1. Henry David Thoreau, *The Journal, 1837–1861* (New York: The New York Review of Books, 2009), 372.

2. Sarah Watts, *Rough Rider in the White House* (Chicago: University of Chicago Press, 2003), 123–35.

3. Photos of Theodore Roosevelt courtesy of the Theodore Roosevelt Collection, Harvard College Library.

4. Watts, 123–35.

5. Ibid.

6. Ibid.

7. Photos of Theodore Roosevelt courtesy of the Theodore Roosevelt Collection, Harvard College Library.

8. Robert Bly, *Iron John* (New York: Vintage Books, 1992), 59.

9. Mary Sykes Wylie, "Panning for Gold (on Michael White)," European Family Therapy Association, http://www.eftacim.org/doc_pdf/mary-sykeswylie.pdf.

10. Bly, 60.

11. Richard Rohr, *Adam's Return* (New York: The Crossroad Publishing Company, 2004), 14.

12. Ibid., 17.

13. Richard Rohr, *Men and Power* (Albuquerque, NM: Center for Action and Contemplation, 2007), CD-ROM.

14. Bly, 70.

15. Ibid., 69–70.

16. Eugene Peterson, *Leap Over a Wall* (New York: HarperCollins, 1997), 27.

17. Richard Rohr, *Men and Grief* (Albuquerque, NM: Center for Action and Contemplation, 2005), CD-ROM.

18. Jean-Jacques Rousseau, *Emile* (New York: D. Appleton Company, 1893), 47.

19. John Eldredge, *The Way of the Wild at Heart* (Nashville: Thomas Nelson, 2006), 83.

20. Leonard Sax, *Boys Adrift* (New York: Basic Books, 2007), 32. This and subsequent quotations from this source are Copyright © 2009 Leonard Sax. Reprinted by permission of Basic Books, a member of the Perseus Books Group.

21. Ibid., 28.

22. David G. Brenner, *Sacred Compaions* (Downers Grove, IL: IVP Books, 2002), 33.

23. Eldredge, 72.

24. Bly, 95–96.

25. David Petersen, editor, *A Hunter's Heart* (New York: Henry Holt and Co., 1996), 92.

26. Alfred Edersheim, *The Temple* (Peabody, MA: Hendrickson Publishers, 1994), 75.

27. Petersen, 29–30.

28. Bly, 29–30.

29. Sax, 124–125.

30. Bly, 69–70.

31. Thomas Aquinas, *Summa Theologica,* public domain.

32. Saint Augustine, *On the Trinity,* public domain.

33. Lee Hardy, *The Fabric of This World* (Grand Rapids, MI: William B. Eerdmans, 1990), 9–10.

34. Jose Luis Illanes, *The Sanctification of Work* (New York: Scepter Publishers, 2003), 41.

35. Hardy, 9–10.

36. Tim Keller, *Before the Beginning* (Redeemer Presbyterian Church, 2008), 34 min., 46 sec., MP3, http://sermons.redeemer.com/store/index.cfm?fuseaction=product.display&Product_ID=18865.

37. Henry David Thoreau, *Walden,* public domain.

38. Elizabeth Gilbert, *Last American Man* (New York: Pengiun Books, 2002), 4.

39. Wendell Berry, *The Unsettling of America* (San Francisco: Sierra Club Books, 1986), 100.

40. Edmund Carpenter, *Arctic Dreams* (New York: Charles Scriber's Sons, 1986), foreword.

41. Harry Middleton, *The Earth is Enough* (Boulder, CO: Pruett Publishing Company, 1996), 44.

42. Berry, 44.

43. Ibid., 53.

44. Rohr, *Adam's Return,* 83.

45. Ibid.

46. Dave Leinweber, e-mail message to author, March 2008.

47. Middleton, 96.

Acknowledgments

There are many folks I am grateful and indebted to who contributed to this book.

I first must thank John Blase for his belief, creativity, and editing. And the crew at David C. Cook: Erin Prater, Doug Mann, Don Pape, Karen Stoller, Amy Quicksall, and Mike Ruman, as well as Joel Kneedler, my wonderful agent at Alive. Thanks for believing in the project.

To my wife: What a brave woman to endure the cost of my many projects! I love you a lot. And I owe you a lot.

To my partner at TG, Cory: We have been through it. Times ten. Many of these stories are because of your invitation.

And to all my good friends in Colorado: Charlton, Sam, P.J., Aaron, Joel, Brett, Nathan, Ryan, Thomas, and Steven—thanks.

An additional thanks to the TG guides and staff. So glad to be with you, leading young men into streams and fields of life.

To the crew at Painter Ready: Carlos, Juan Carlos, Jack, John, Jesse, Cory, and Mike—thanks for teaching this entitled boy the areas of life I could not have learned in books.

All the reps for Buffalo & Company and Campbell who are eager to build a company that's all about what clothes are meant to be—thanks.

A great big thanks to the guys of Blood and Dirt who offered their generous thoughts and wisdom to these rough words as I wrote.

To my parents: I know you endure my vulnerability with your seat belts fastened, but I pray for smiles along the way as we walk it out. I am glad to be your son.

And to my brother, Zac. There are miles to go before we sleep.

I also must thank all those with whom I had good conversations about this book and have been so kind to invest in me: John, David, Richard, Gus, Krue, Cal, Jimmy, Joni, Jan, Dan, Cathie, Lynn, Sam, and Cory.

And those from whom I gleaned firsthand inspiration and knowledge in work and wilderness—Timm, Ron, Earl, Jere, Richard, Jeremy, Steve, Mark, Charles, and Dan—many thanks. I also must mention that I learned a lot through the books of Walt Harrington, Richard Rohr, John Eldredge, Robert Bly, Steven Rinella, Harry Middleton, Leonard Sax, John Muir, Teddy Roosevelt, Wendell Berry, and Elizabeth Gilbert.

And to our Father in heaven: Thanks for giving a man a fish when he finally asked. I pray it will feed others.